I0458417

THE
EVERYDAY
PHILOSOPHER

Timeless Ideas for Modern Problems

FELIX GRAYSON

MINDSPARK
PUBLISHING

To the seekers of meaning and the builders of connection— May your journey be guided by curiosity, courage, and purpose.

"What lies behind us and what lies before us are tiny matters compared to what lies within us."

— *Ralph Waldo Emerson*

ABOUT STONED PHILOSOPHER

Welcome to the *Stoned Philosopher* series—where timeless wisdom meets the modern world.

Each book distills powerful lessons from history's greatest minds, leaders, and thinkers—transforming their ideas into practical insights for today's challenges.

From mastering habits, calm, and resilience to understanding success, leadership, and meaning, this collection invites you to think deeper, live wiser, and see life from new perspectives.

Whether you're exploring *Modern Zen*, uncovering *The Wisdom of Warriors*, or seeking clarity through *The Art of Perspective*, every title offers a journey toward self-mastery and understanding.

Discover the full *Stoned Philosopher* collection and more at **FelixGrayson.com**, home of **Mind-Spark Publishing**—where knowledge, philosophy, and storytelling come together to spark lifelong curiosity.

FelixGrayson.com

Wisdom isn't something we find—it's something we grow into.

Let the journey begin.

CONTENTS

INTRODUCTION: BECOMING THE EVERYDAY PHILOSOPHER

Life often feels like a rush — an endless series of tasks, obligations, and distractions. In the midst of this whirlwind, it's easy to lose sight of the deeper questions: *What truly matters? What kind of life do I want to live? How can I create meaning, even in the ordinary?* These questions are not new; they have echoed through centuries, posed by philosophers, leaders, and everyday thinkers who sought to understand the essence of life. Their answers, though rooted in different times and contexts, remain timeless, offering a wellspring of wisdom for those willing to listen.

This book, *The Everyday Philosopher*, is your invitation to listen.

Philosophy has long been perceived as something lofty and inaccessible, confined to ivory towers or ancient texts. Yet at its heart, philosophy is about life—how we think, how we act, and how we find meaning in the everyday. It is not reserved for scholars or sages; it is for anyone who seeks to live thoughtfully and intentionally. You don't need to wear a toga or master Socratic dialogue to embrace philosophy; you simply need curiosity, courage, and a willingness to ask, How can I live better?

Why Philosophy Matters Today

In an era defined by constant change and unprecedented challenges, philosophy is more relevant than ever. The questions we face—how to navigate uncertainty, build resilience, find balance, and connect with others—are universal, transcending time and culture. The answers, too, are universal, offering guiding principles that empower us to thrive in the face of adversity and complexity.

Philosophy matters because it grounds us. In a world where we are inundated with information, where technology accelerates every aspect of life, and where external pressures often dictate our choices, philosophy reminds us to pause, reflect, and align our actions with our values. It teaches us that we are not merely products of circumstance but active participants in shaping our lives.

Consider the wisdom of Marcus Aurelius, the Roman emperor who wrote, "You have power over your mind—not outside events. Realize this, and you will find strength." His words, penned over 2,000 years ago, resonate just as strongly today, offering a blueprint for resilience in the face of life's unpredictability. This is the gift of philosophy: it provides tools to navigate not only the extraordinary but also the mundane, transforming daily life into a canvas for growth, connection, and purpose.

The Themes That Guide Us

The Everyday Philosopher is structured around themes that address the fundamental aspects of a meaningful life: resilience, balance, purpose, relationships, and ethics. Each chapter explores these concepts through the lens of timeless wisdom, blending historical insights with practical applications that are relevant to modern life.

Resilience teaches us how to endure and grow

through adversity, finding strength in even the most challenging circumstances. Balance reminds us that harmony is not about perfection but about aligning our priorities in a way that sustains us. Purpose gives us a sense of direction, helping us see beyond the daily grind to the legacy we want to leave. Relationships enrich our lives, teaching us the value of empathy, trust, and meaningful connection. And ethics challenges us to live with integrity, ensuring that our actions reflect our highest values.

These themes are not isolated; they are interconnected, forming a holistic framework for living with intention. Together, they empower us to navigate the complexities of life with clarity and confidence, transforming ordinary moments into opportunities for growth and fulfillment.

What You Can Expect

This is not a book of abstract ideas or philosophical jargon. It is a practical guide—a conversation between you and the thinkers who have shaped the world's understanding of what it means to live well. Each chapter is designed to provide both inspiration and action, combining timeless insights with tools you can apply to your own life.

You will encounter stories of historical figures like Viktor Frankl, who found meaning in the midst of unimaginable suffering, and Aristotle, whose teachings on habits continue to influence our understanding of self-discipline and character. You will also find reflections on everyday challenges, from managing stress and maintaining balance to navigating ethical dilemmas and building meaningful connections.

The goal of this book is not to give you all the answers but to spark the questions that matter most. It invites you to reflect on your own life, to examine your values, and to consider how you can live in greater alignment with them. It is a journey, and like any meaningful journey, it will require curiosity, courage, and an open mind.

A Personal Invitation

Before we dive in, I want to share something personal. Like many of you, I have wrestled with questions about purpose, balance, and resilience. I have faced moments of uncertainty, conflict, and doubt, wondering if I was on the right path. It was during these moments that I turned to the wisdom of the past—not as an escape but as a guide. I found comfort in the words of Marcus Aurelius, clarity in the teachings of Confucius, and courage in the example of figures like Gandhi and Eleanor Roosevelt.

This book is a product of that journey. It is a collection of lessons that have not only shaped my thinking but also transformed my life. Writing it has been an act of reflection and gratitude—a way to honor the thinkers who have inspired me and to share their wisdom with you. My hope is that these pages will serve as a companion on your own journey, offering guidance, encouragement, and a sense of possibility.

Your Role as the Everyday Philosopher

At its core, this book is about empowerment. It is about recognizing that you have the capacity to live thoughtfully, intentionally, and meaningfully, no matter your circumstances. You are not a passive observer of life; you are its author. Every choice you make, every action you take, contributes to the story of who you are and the legacy you leave.

As you read, I encourage you to approach this book not as a set of instructions but as a dialogue. Reflect on what resonates with you, challenge what doesn't, and consider how these ideas can shape your own philosophy of living. The goal is not to adopt someone else's way of thinking but to develop your own—a way of thinking that aligns with your values and aspirations.

The title of this book, *The Everyday Philosopher*, is not a label; it is an invitation. It invites you to see philosophy not as a distant discipline but as a daily practice. It invites you to ask questions, seek meaning, and find wisdom in the ordinary. And most importantly, it invites you to embrace the journey of becoming—not a perfect philosopher, but an intentional one.

The Journey Ahead

As we embark on this journey together, let me leave you with one final thought: life is not a problem to be solved but a mystery to be lived. The answers we seek are not always clear, but the questions themselves are worth asking. By engaging with these questions—about resilience, balance, purpose, relationships, and ethics—we create a life that is not only rich in meaning but also deeply connected to the world around us.

This book is your guide, but the journey is yours. I invite you to step into it with curiosity, courage, and an open heart. Together, let us explore what it means to live as the *Everyday Philosopher*. Let us discover the wisdom that lies within and the possibilities that lie ahead.

CHAPTER 1: FOUNDATIONS OF WISDOM – UNDERSTANDING TIMELESS TRUTHS

The Search for Truth Across Time

Humanity's pursuit of truth is as ancient as civilization itself, a journey that has defined our cultures, shaped our philosophies, and enriched our understanding of existence. Across centuries and continents, individuals have sought to unravel life's mysteries, asking fundamental questions about meaning, purpose, and the nature of reality. From the probing dialogues of Socratic Athens to the introspective meditations of the East, this shared quest underscores a universal yearning to connect with something greater than ourselves.

Socrates and the Courage to Question

The search for truth often begins with the Greeks, whose philosophers laid the foundation for critical inquiry. Socrates, a cornerstone of this tradition, dared to question the assumptions of his peers, relentlessly pursuing a deeper understanding of virtue, justice, and the good life. For Socrates, truth was not a static concept to be memorized but a dynamic process of discovery, achieved through persistent questioning and dialogue.

His Socratic Method, characterized by asking and answering questions to stimulate critical thinking, remains a powerful tool for navigating modern complexities. Socrates believed that the pursuit of truth required humility, as individuals must confront their ignorance before they can achieve enlightenment. In his own words, "I know that I know nothing," a declaration that invites us to approach the world with curiosity and openness.

In today's world, where misinformation and echo chambers often dominate discourse, Socratic questioning reminds us of the importance of intellectual honesty. By challenging surface-level assumptions and probing deeper into the heart of issues, we can cultivate a more nuanced understanding of ourselves and the world around us.

The Inner Journey: Truth in Eastern Traditions

While Socrates emphasized dialogue and outward inquiry, ancient Indian and Chinese philosophies turned inward, seeking truth through self-awareness and harmony. The Upanishads, a collection of foundational Hindu texts, explore the relationship between the self (*Atman*) and the ultimate reality (*Brahman*). According to these teachings, the path to truth involves transcending material distractions and recognizing the interconnectedness of all existence.

This concept of unity resonates deeply with modern readers navigating an often fragmented world. The Upanishads remind us that truth is not something to be acquired externally but something to be uncovered within ourselves. By practicing mindfulness and introspection, we can peel back the layers of ego and illusion to discover our authentic nature.

Buddhism, too, offers profound insights into the search for truth, particularly through the Four Noble Truths and the Eightfold Path. The Buddha taught that suffering arises from attachment and that liberation lies in cultivating wisdom, ethical conduct, and mental discipline. These teachings encourage us to let go of superficial desires and focus on enduring truths—principles that remain relevant as we grapple with the stresses of modern life.

In China, Confucius approached truth through the lens of relationships and social harmony. His teachings emphasized the importance of virtues like *ren* (benevolence) and *li* (proper conduct), which promote balance within both the individual and the community. For Confucius, truth was not an abstract ideal but a lived experience, embodied through ethical behavior and respect for tradition. His philosophy reminds us that the search for truth is not only personal but also communal, as our actions ripple outward to shape the world around us.

Bridging Past and Present: Truth in a Modern Context

The challenges of pursuing truth in the modern era are distinct from those faced by ancient philosophers. Today, we live in an age of information overload, where countless voices compete for our attention and countless platforms amplify noise over substance. The proliferation of social media, 24-hour news cycles, and algorithm-driven content has created an environment where truth often feels elusive.

Yet the timeless teachings of Socrates, the Upanishads, and Confucius offer invaluable guidance for navigating this complexity. Socrates' emphasis on questioning remains a vital skill for discerning fact from fiction in a digital world. By approaching information critically and refusing to accept claims at face value, we can sift through the noise to uncover deeper truths.

Meanwhile, the introspective practices of Eastern philosophy—such as meditation, mindful breathing, and journaling—can help us reconnect with our inner compass amid external distractions. These practices create space for reflection, enabling us to distinguish between fleeting desires and enduring values. Confucius' focus on ethical relationships also resonates today, reminding us that truth is not just about personal enlightenment but also about fostering trust, respect, and understanding in our communities.

The Timeless Relevance of Truth-Seeking

Despite the differences between ancient and modern contexts, the essence of the search for truth remains unchanged: it is a journey of questioning, learning, and growth. Socrates, the Upanishadic sages, and Confucius each approached this journey from unique perspectives, yet their teachings converge on a shared principle—that truth is transformative. It shapes how we think, how we act, and how we relate to others.

In the words of the Buddha, "Three things cannot be long hidden: the sun, the moon, and the truth." This insight speaks to the enduring power of truth to illuminate our lives, even in the darkest of times. By embracing the wisdom of the past and applying it to the challenges of the present, we can move closer to a life of authenticity, clarity, and purpose.

As we continue this journey in the chapters ahead, let us keep in mind the lessons of these great thinkers. They remind us that truth is not a destination but a practice, one that requires patience, courage, and humility. Whether through Socratic questioning, Eastern introspection, or the ethical frameworks of Confucianism, the search for truth remains a timeless and vital pursuit, connecting us to the wisdom of the ages and to one another.

Core Philosophical Concepts for Modern Life

The human experience is marked by a relentless pursuit of meaning—a desire to understand what it means to live a good life. Over centuries, philosophers have articulated concepts that resonate across cultures and eras, offering frameworks for navigating the challenges of existence. Virtue, justice, and the pursuit of happiness are among the most enduring of these ideas, forming the cornerstones of both personal growth and societal harmony. Despite their ancient origins, these concepts remain deeply relevant, providing practical guidance for the complexities of modern life.

Virtue: The Foundation of Character

For ancient Greek philosophers like Aristotle, virtue was the cornerstone of a life well-lived. In his *Nicomachean Ethics*, Aristotle described virtue as a state of character achieved by practicing moral excellence. He argued that virtues such as courage, temperance, and generosity lie at the "Golden Mean," the balance between deficiency and excess. For example, courage is the mean between cowardice and recklessness, while generosity is the mean between stinginess and extravagance. By striving for this balance, individuals cultivate habits that align their actions with their values.

The concept of virtue transcends time because it focuses on the cultivation of character rather than fleeting achievements. In a world increasingly obsessed with external markers of success— wealth, fame, and social validation—Aristotle's emphasis on internal growth feels particularly poignant. Modern readers can apply this idea by reflecting on their own virtues: Are my actions guided by integrity? Do I consistently strive to do what is right, even when it is difficult? These questions encourage a shift from superficial measures of worth to a deeper examination of who we are and who we aspire to be.

Incorporating virtue into daily life requires conscious effort and self-awareness. For instance, practicing patience in stressful situations or demonstrating kindness to those in need are small but significant ways to embody virtue.

Over time, these practices become ingrained, shaping not only individual character but also the collective ethos of a community.

Justice: The Pursuit of Fairness

Justice, a principle that has shaped civilizations, reflects humanity's innate desire for fairness and equality. Plato explored this concept in *The Republic*, where he described justice as a harmony between the individual and the state. For Plato, a just society is one in which everyone fulfills their rightful role, contributing to the greater good while respecting the rights of others. This vision of justice emphasizes both individual responsibility and collective well-being.

Centuries later, the Enlightenment thinker John Rawls expanded on the idea of justice, framing it as fairness. In his seminal work *A Theory of Justice*, Rawls proposed the "veil of ignorance" thought experiment, asking individuals to imagine themselves designing a society without knowing their own social position. This perspective encourages the creation of systems that prioritize equity, ensuring that even the most vulnerable members of society are protected.

In contemporary life, justice manifests in various ways, from advocating for social equality to addressing ethical dilemmas in the workplace. It challenges us to look beyond personal gain and consider the broader implications of our actions. For example, when faced with a decision that affects others—whether at work, in relationships, or within the community—applying the principle of justice involves asking: Is this fair? Does this uphold the dignity of all involved?

Justice also plays a critical role in fostering trust and collaboration. When people perceive fairness in their interactions and institutions, they are more likely to engage meaningfully and contribute positively. By embracing justice as a guiding principle, individuals can help create environments that are not only equitable but also deeply enriching.

The Pursuit of Happiness: A Timeless Aspiration

Happiness, perhaps the most universal of

human desires, has been a central theme in philosophical discourse for centuries. Aristotle identified happiness, or *eudaimonia*, as the ultimate goal of life—a state of flourishing achieved through virtuous living and the fulfillment of one's potential. This concept differs from fleeting pleasures or material satisfaction, focusing instead on long-term well-being and meaningful engagement with life.

Eastern traditions echo this sentiment, emphasizing contentment and inner peace as pathways to happiness. The teachings of Buddhism, for example, highlight the importance of letting go of attachments and cultivating mindfulness. The Buddha's Four Noble Truths suggest that true happiness arises not from external circumstances but from mastering one's own mind.

In a modern context, the pursuit of happiness often feels complicated by societal pressures and the constant comparison fostered by social media. Advertisements promise fulfillment through consumerism, while cultural narratives equate success with happiness. Yet, as ancient wisdom suggests, true happiness lies not in what we acquire but in how we live. Cultivating gratitude, practicing mindfulness, and building meaningful relationships are practical steps toward achieving a deeper, more sustainable sense of joy.

Happiness, like virtue and justice, requires intentional effort. It invites us to reflect on what truly brings us joy and align our lives with those values. Whether through acts of kindness, moments of self-care, or the pursuit of meaningful goals, the journey toward happiness is as transformative as the destination itself.

Bringing Timeless Concepts into Modern Practice

Virtue, justice, and the pursuit of happiness are not abstract ideals confined to philosophical texts; they are practical tools for navigating the complexities of modern life. By grounding our actions in these principles, we create a framework for personal growth, ethical decision-making, and meaningful engagement with the world.

Consider a scenario where these concepts intersect: a workplace conflict. A virtuous response might involve approaching the situation with empathy and integrity, seeking to understand all perspectives. A commitment to justice ensures that the resolution is fair and inclusive, addressing the needs of everyone involved. And the pursuit of happiness reminds us to prioritize long-term harmony over short-term victories, fostering a positive environment that benefits both individuals and the collective.

These principles also encourage us to approach life with a sense of purpose. Virtue inspires us to be our best selves, justice connects us to the broader community, and happiness motivates us to find joy in the journey. Together, they form a foundation for living with intention, resilience, and authenticity.

As we reflect on these timeless ideas, it becomes clear that their relevance transcends the ages. They challenge us to think deeply, act ethically, and pursue meaning in a world that often feels chaotic. By integrating these concepts into our daily lives, we honor the wisdom of the past while building a future defined by clarity, purpose, and fulfillment.

Philosophy as a Practical Tool

Philosophy, often perceived as an abstract pursuit, is far more than intellectual musing; it is a profoundly practical tool for navigating the challenges of life. From ancient thinkers like Marcus Aurelius and Confucius to modern philosophers such as Martha Nussbaum, the enduring appeal of philosophy lies in its ability to equip us with clarity, resilience, and ethical grounding. By applying philosophical thinking to decision-making, problem-solving, and self-awareness, we can transform how we approach both the mundane and the extraordinary.

The Role of Philosophy in Decision-Making

Every decision we make, whether large or small, shapes the trajectory of our lives. Philosophical reasoning offers a structured way to approach these choices with greater clarity and intentionality. For instance, the Stoics, particularly Marcus Aurelius, emphasized the importance of focusing on what lies within our control. In his *Meditations*, Marcus reminds us that external events are beyond our influence, but our responses to them are entirely ours to govern. This perspective shifts the decision-making process from one of frustration or fear to one of empowerment.

Imagine being faced with a difficult career decision, such as whether to accept a promotion that may disrupt your work-life balance. A Stoic approach would involve calmly assessing the factors within your control—your skills, values, and priorities—while accepting the uncertainty inherent in the outcome. By grounding decisions in reason rather than emotion, philosophy helps us act with confidence, even in the face of ambiguity.

Ethical reasoning, another hallmark of philosophical thinking, is equally vital in decision-making. Immanuel Kant's concept of the *categorical imperative*—to act in a way that you would will to become universal law—provides a powerful framework for evaluating choices. This principle encourages us to consider not just the immediate consequences of our actions but their broader moral implications. For example, when deciding how to handle a conflict at work, Kantian ethics might prompt us to ask:

Am I treating others with respect and fairness? Would I endorse my approach as a standard for others? These questions guide us toward decisions that align with our values and contribute to the greater good.

Philosophy as a Guide to Problem-Solving

Life's challenges often feel overwhelming because they seem insurmountable or devoid of clear solutions. Philosophy offers tools to reframe problems, breaking them down into manageable components and uncovering hidden opportunities for growth. The pragmatist philosopher John Dewey advocated for a problem-solving approach rooted in inquiry and experimentation. Dewey viewed problems not as obstacles but as invitations to engage with the world more thoughtfully.

Consider a personal conflict, such as a strained relationship with a friend or family member. Dewey's method would encourage you to analyze the underlying issues objectively, explore potential solutions, and test them iteratively. Perhaps the conflict arises from miscommunication; addressing this might involve open dialogue and active listening. By treating the problem as a puzzle to be solved rather than a burden to be endured, philosophical thinking transforms adversity into a catalyst for improvement.

The Buddhist concept of *right effort*, part of the Eightfold Path, also informs problem-solving. This principle emphasizes the importance of channeling energy toward constructive actions while avoiding futile or harmful pursuits. In practice, this means focusing on what can be changed and letting go of unproductive worry or blame. Applying this mindset to challenges—whether professional setbacks or personal disappointments—fosters resilience and clarity, enabling us to act purposefully.

Philosophy and Self-Awareness

Self-awareness is the cornerstone of personal growth, and philosophy offers profound insights into understanding ourselves more deeply. Socrates' dictum, "Know thyself," underscores the importance of introspection in leading an authentic life. Philosophical reflection encourages us to examine our beliefs, motivations, and behaviors, revealing patterns that may hinder or enhance our well-being.

For example, the concept of *bad faith*, explored by existentialist Jean-Paul Sartre, refers to the tendency to deceive ourselves about our choices and responsibilities. Sartre argued that individuals often conform to societal expectations or external pressures rather than embracing their freedom to define their own paths. Recognizing and challenging these tendencies is a key step toward living authentically.

Mindfulness, rooted in Buddhist philosophy, also plays a crucial role in cultivating self-awareness. By observing our thoughts and emotions without judgment, we gain insight into the forces that drive our actions. This practice not only deepens our understanding of ourselves but also helps us respond to life's challenges with greater composure and wisdom. For instance, recognizing a pattern of reactive anger in stressful situations allows us to pause, reflect, and choose a more constructive response.

Building Resilience Through Philosophical

Thinking

Resilience—the ability to adapt and thrive in the face of adversity—is perhaps one of the most valuable outcomes of applying philosophy to daily life. Stoicism, with its emphasis on inner strength and equanimity, offers timeless strategies for building resilience. Seneca, a prominent Stoic thinker, advised embracing life's hardships as opportunities to develop courage and fortitude. "Difficulties strengthen the mind," he wrote, "as labor does the body."

Modern applications of this idea might include reframing failures as learning experiences or viewing setbacks as temporary rather than definitive. For example, a failed business venture can be seen not as a personal defeat but as a valuable lesson in perseverance and adaptability. By adopting a philosophical perspective, we learn to navigate challenges with grace and determination.

Philosophy also fosters resilience by helping us find meaning in suffering. Viktor Frankl, a Holocaust survivor and existential psychologist, explored this idea in his book *Man's Search for*

Meaning. Frankl argued that even in the most harrowing circumstances, individuals can find purpose by focusing on what truly matters— whether through love, creative work, or acts of kindness. This insight empowers us to endure difficulties with a sense of hope and purpose, transforming hardship into a source of strength.

Philosophy as a Practical Compass

Ultimately, philosophy serves as a compass, guiding us through the complexities of modern life with wisdom and clarity. Whether we are navigating ethical dilemmas, resolving conflicts, or confronting personal challenges, philosophical thinking provides tools to act thoughtfully and authentically. It encourages us to approach life not as a series of disconnected events but as a coherent narrative shaped by our values and choices.

By integrating philosophical principles into our daily routines, we can cultivate greater resilience, self-awareness, and ethical grounding. Whether through Stoic reflections, Buddhist mindfulness, or Kantian ethics, these timeless tools remind us that we are not passive participants in life but active agents of our own stories. In the face of uncertainty, philosophy offers not just answers but the courage to ask better questions—and in doing so, it equips us to thrive.

Wisdom in Action – Everyday Applications

The greatest value of philosophical wisdom lies in its ability to shape how we live our daily lives. Philosophy is not merely a set of abstract theories to ponder but a practical guide for action—a means of navigating life's challenges with clarity, intention, and grace. From the simple act of pausing to reflect before making a decision to cultivating habits that foster inner peace, philosophy offers tools that are both timeless and profoundly relevant. By integrating practices such as journaling, mindful questioning, and reflection into our routines, we can embody wisdom in action and transform even the most ordinary moments into opportunities for growth.

Journaling as a Tool for Self-Reflection

Journaling, a practice embraced by philosophers throughout history, remains one of the most effective ways to apply wisdom in everyday life. Marcus Aurelius, the Roman emperor and Stoic philosopher, famously used his personal journal to examine his thoughts, reflect on his actions, and reaffirm his principles. His *Meditations*, originally intended for his eyes only, offers a glimpse into the power of this practice. Through journaling, Marcus was able to confront his fears, clarify his values, and navigate the immense pressures of leadership with equanimity.

In modern life, journaling serves a similar purpose. By setting aside time to write, we create a space for introspection—a chance to step back from the chaos of daily life and engage in meaningful self-dialogue. For example, journaling can help us process difficult emotions, identify patterns in our behavior, and explore solutions to recurring challenges. A simple practice might involve starting each day by writing down three intentions or ending the evening by reflecting on what went well and what could be improved.

The act of putting thoughts into words fosters self-awareness, making it easier to align our actions with our values. Over time, journaling becomes a tool not only for self-discovery but also for cultivating resilience and clarity, enabling us to face life's uncertainties with greater confidence.

Mindful Questioning: The Art of Asking Better Questions

At the heart of philosophical inquiry lies the art of questioning—an approach that can be transformative when applied to our daily lives. Socrates, the father of this method, believed that asking the right questions was more important than having the right answers. His technique, known as the Socratic Method, encouraged deep exploration by challenging assumptions and probing the underlying beliefs that shape our decisions.

Mindful questioning invites us to adopt this practice in our own lives. For instance, when faced with a difficult situation, we might ask ourselves: What truly matters in this moment? What am I assuming about this problem? How might I approach this differently? These questions shift our focus from reacting impulsively to responding thoughtfully, helping us uncover insights that might otherwise go unnoticed.

Consider a moment of conflict, whether at work or in a personal relationship. Rather than jumping to conclusions or assigning blame, mindful questioning encourages us to pause and reflect: What does the other person need right now? How can I communicate with empathy? By fostering curiosity and openness, this practice transforms conflict into an opportunity for understanding and growth.

Reflection and the Power of Pause

In a world that values speed and efficiency, the simple act of pausing can feel revolutionary. Yet, reflection is essential for integrating wisdom into action. Philosophical traditions across cultures emphasize the importance of creating space for stillness, whether through meditation, prayer, or quiet contemplation. These moments of pause allow us to step back, observe our thoughts, and reconnect with our deeper intentions.

The Buddhist practice of mindfulness offers a powerful framework for cultivating reflection in daily life. By focusing on the present moment without judgment, mindfulness helps us become more attuned to our inner experiences and external surroundings. For example, during a stressful meeting, pausing to take a few mindful breaths can help us respond with composure rather than reacting emotionally. Similarly, setting aside time each evening to reflect on the day's events fosters a sense of closure and prepares us to approach the next day with renewed clarity.

Reflection also enhances our ability to learn from experience. As Confucius observed, "By three methods we may learn wisdom: First, by reflection, which is noblest; Second, by imitation, which is easiest; and third, by experience, which is bitterest." By taking the time to reflect, we transform even our mistakes into valuable lessons, equipping ourselves to make wiser choices in the future.

Habits as Vehicles for Wisdom

Wisdom is not just something we think about; it is something we live. The philosopher Aristotle believed that excellence is achieved through habit—that by consistently practicing virtues such as patience, kindness, and honesty, we become virtuous people. In his view, small, intentional actions repeated over time shape our character and determine the quality of our lives.

This principle can be applied to modern routines in countless ways. For instance, starting the day with a moment of gratitude, committing to a regular exercise routine, or practicing active listening in conversations are all habits that embody philosophical wisdom. These actions may seem small, but their cumulative impact is profound. By embedding wisdom into our habits, we ensure that our values are not confined to lofty ideals but are reflected in the way we live each day.

One practical approach is to use habit-stacking, a technique popularized by modern behavioral psychology. This involves linking a new habit to an existing routine, making it easier to integrate into daily life. For example, pairing a gratitude practice with your morning coffee or adding a moment of mindful breathing before your evening commute transforms ordinary moments into opportunities for growth.

Living Philosophy in the Everyday

Perhaps the greatest gift of philosophy is its ability to elevate the ordinary. Wisdom in action is not about grand gestures or dramatic transformations; it is about the choices we make moment by moment. It is the decision to listen deeply when a friend shares their struggles, to approach a challenge with curiosity rather than fear, to pause and reflect before speaking in anger. These small acts, repeated daily, accumulate into a life of meaning and purpose.

The teachings of the great philosophers remind us that wisdom is not something reserved for scholars or sages—it is available to all who seek it. By journaling, questioning, reflecting, and cultivating habits that align with our values, we bring philosophy to life in ways that are practical, accessible, and deeply transformative. In doing so, we honor the timeless truths of the past while creating a brighter, more intentional future for ourselves and those around us.

CHAPTER 2:
THE POWER OF
PERSPECTIVE –
SHIFTING YOUR
MINDSET

The Philosophy of Perception

Our perception of the world profoundly influences how we experience it. This idea, central to both ancient philosophy and modern psychology, suggests that events themselves hold no inherent meaning—it is our interpretation of them that shapes our reality. The power of perception lies in its ability to transform adversity into opportunity, despair into hope, and confusion into clarity. Philosophers like Epictetus and Viktor Frankl have explored this transformative potential, reminding us that while we cannot always control our circumstances, we can control how we perceive and respond to them.

Epictetus: Mastering the Mind's Lens

The Stoic philosopher Epictetus famously observed, "Men are disturbed not by things, but by the views they take of them." In his teachings, Epictetus emphasized that external events are beyond our control, but our perceptions of those events are entirely within our power. He urged his followers to focus on what they could influence—their thoughts, actions, and attitudes—rather than becoming entangled in frustration over uncontrollable circumstances.

Consider a modern parallel: a missed flight. For one person, this might be a catastrophe, triggering anger and stress about disrupted plans. For another, it could be a chance to pause, reflect, and even explore the unexpected opportunities of an extended layover. The event itself—the missed flight—remains the same, but the experience diverges dramatically based on how it is perceived. Epictetus invites us to cultivate a mindset that reframes such challenges, viewing them not as obstacles but as opportunities to practice patience, resilience, and adaptability.

In practical terms, adopting this Stoic perspective begins with mindfulness. When faced with a difficult situation, pause to examine your initial reaction: Is this response helping or hindering me? What aspect of this situation is within my control? By shifting focus from what you cannot change to what you can, you regain a sense of agency and clarity, even in the midst of uncertainty.

Viktor Frankl: Finding Meaning in Suffering

The transformative power of perception is perhaps most poignantly illustrated in the life and work of Viktor Frankl, a Holocaust survivor and psychiatrist. In his seminal book, *Man's Search for Meaning*, Frankl recounts his experiences in Nazi concentration camps and the profound realization that even in the direst circumstances, individuals retain the freedom to choose their attitude.

Frankl observed that those who survived the camps were often those who could find meaning in their suffering. For some, this meaning came from a sense of responsibility to others, whether it was caring for a fellow prisoner or holding onto the hope of reuniting with loved ones. For others, it came from a commitment to a greater purpose, such as faith, art, or the desire to bear witness to humanity's resilience.

Frankl's philosophy centers on the idea that life's meaning is not dictated by external conditions but is something we create through our perceptions and choices. He wrote, "When we are no longer able to change a situation, we are challenged to change ourselves." This perspective offers a powerful antidote to despair, reminding us that even in moments of profound loss or suffering, we can find purpose and strength by reframing our experience.

Applying Frankl's insights to modern life involves asking ourselves purposeful questions: What lesson can I learn from this challenge? How can I use this experience to grow? Who might benefit from my resilience or example? These questions shift our focus from the pain of the moment to the possibilities that lie beyond it, empowering us to navigate adversity with courage and intention.

The Science of Framing: Shaping Reality Through Perspective

While philosophy provides the foundation for understanding perception, modern psychology offers complementary insights into how framing shapes our experience of reality. The concept of "cognitive framing" refers to the mental structures we use to interpret information. How we frame an event influences not only our emotional response but also our subsequent actions.

Research in positive psychology highlights the power of reframing to improve well-being. For instance, studies have shown that individuals who focus on the silver linings of challenging experiences report higher levels of resilience and life satisfaction. This principle is exemplified by the "growth mindset," which encourages viewing setbacks as opportunities for learning rather than failures. A student who receives critical feedback on a project, for example, might frame it as an opportunity to improve and succeed in the future, rather than as evidence of inadequacy.

Reframing can be practiced in simple but impactful ways. Imagine a stressful work deadline. Instead of focusing on the pressure, you might frame it as an opportunity to demonstrate your skills and creativity. Similarly, a difficult conversation with a loved one can be reframed as a chance to deepen understanding and strengthen the relationship. By consciously choosing how we frame situations, we cultivate a more empowering and constructive mindset.

Perspective as a Daily Practice

Shifting perspective is not a one-time event but a practice—a habit of the mind that requires intentional effort. This practice begins with awareness, the ability to recognize when our perceptions are limiting us. Journaling, meditation, or simply taking a moment to pause and reflect can help cultivate this awareness.

Once we are aware of our perceptions, we can begin to challenge and reframe them. This process might involve asking questions such as: Is there another way to view this situation? What strengths or opportunities might this challenge reveal? How would I advise a friend in a similar position? These questions create mental space to explore alternative perspectives, breaking free from the automatic responses that often dominate our thinking.

The benefits of this practice extend beyond personal growth. Perspective shapes how we interact with others, fostering empathy and understanding. By acknowledging that each person views the world through their own unique lens, we approach relationships with greater compassion and openness. This shift not only enhances our connections but also enriches our collective ability to navigate shared challenges.

The Transformative Power of Perception

The philosophy of perception teaches us that our reality is not fixed but fluid, shaped by the stories we tell ourselves and the meanings we assign to events. Epictetus and Viktor Frankl remind us that we have the power to choose these stories, even in the face of adversity. By reframing challenges, finding meaning in suffering, and cultivating a mindset of growth and possibility, we transform not only how we experience life but also how we contribute to the world around us.

As we carry these lessons forward, the question becomes: How will we choose to perceive the world? The answer, as philosophy and psychology alike suggest, holds the key to a life of clarity, resilience, and profound fulfillment.

Gratitude and Impermanence

In the midst of life's uncertainty and change, gratitude offers a grounding force, a way to anchor ourselves in the present and find joy amid the transient nature of existence. At its core, gratitude is more than an emotional response — it is a deliberate practice, a perspective that can transform how we experience the world. Both Buddhist and Stoic traditions emphasize the importance of embracing impermanence and cultivating gratitude as paths to contentment. Together, these teachings provide timeless wisdom for navigating stress, finding fulfillment, and living more fully in the moment.

Buddhist Teachings: Embracing Impermanence

Central to Buddhist philosophy is the concept of impermanence, or *anicca*. The Buddha taught that everything in life — our possessions, relationships, even our own bodies — is in a constant state of flux. Clinging to permanence in a world that is ever-changing, he observed, is a source of suffering. However, by accepting impermanence, we free ourselves from the pain of attachment and open our hearts to the beauty of the present.

Consider a common source of stress: the fear of loss. Whether it is the loss of a loved one, a job, or a cherished dream, this fear often stems from our desire to hold onto what feels stable and secure. Buddhist philosophy reframes this experience, suggesting that rather than resisting change, we might embrace it as a natural and inevitable part of life. By doing so, we create space for gratitude—not only for what we have but also for the transient nature of those blessings, which makes them all the more precious.

A practical application of this teaching is the practice of mindfulness. Through mindfulness, we learn to observe our thoughts and emotions without judgment, allowing us to acknowledge impermanence without being overwhelmed by it. For instance, when we experience a moment of joy—a laugh shared with a friend, the warmth of the sun on our skin—mindfulness encourages us to savor it fully, knowing it will not last forever. This awareness does not diminish the experience but enhances it, transforming fleeting moments into profound sources of gratitude.

Stoic Wisdom: Gratitude for What Is

The Stoics, like the Buddhists, understood the transient nature of life and the importance of cultivating gratitude in the face of uncertainty. Marcus Aurelius, the Roman emperor and Stoic philosopher, wrote extensively about this in his *Meditations*. "Do not indulge in dreams of having what you do not have," he advised, "but reckon up the chief of the blessings you do possess, and then thankfully remember how you would crave for them if they were not yours."

For the Stoics, gratitude was not about denying life's challenges but about finding value in what already exists. This perspective fosters resilience, helping us shift our focus from what is lacking to what is present and abundant. Imagine facing a difficult day at work. The Stoic approach might involve pausing to appreciate the opportunity to grow, the support of colleagues, or even the simple fact of having a job. By reframing our circumstances in this way, we transform frustration into contentment and scarcity into abundance.

The Stoic practice of negative visualization, or *premeditatio malorum*, offers another tool for fostering gratitude. This involves imagining the loss of something we value—a loved one, a cherished possession, or even our own health—not as a morbid exercise but as a reminder of their importance. By contemplating life without these blessings, we deepen our appreciation for them in the present.

Finding Gratitude Amid Adversity

One of the most powerful aspects of gratitude is its ability to thrive even in adversity. Viktor Frankl, whose experiences in Nazi concentration camps profoundly shaped his philosophy, demonstrated this principle in his own life. Despite enduring unimaginable suffering, Frankl found reasons for gratitude, whether it was a kind word from a fellow prisoner or a fleeting glimpse of beauty in a bleak environment. His perspective serves as a testament to the resilience of the human spirit and the transformative power of gratitude.

In modern life, we often face challenges that, while less extreme, can still feel overwhelming—financial struggles, relationship conflicts, or the stress of balancing work and family. In these moments, gratitude can serve as an anchor, helping us find stability and strength. For example, during a difficult period, reflecting on even small sources of gratitude—a supportive friend, a peaceful moment in nature, or a meal shared with loved ones—can shift our focus from despair to hope.

Practicing gratitude does not mean ignoring or minimizing pain. Instead, it involves holding space for both joy and sorrow, recognizing that they often coexist. This dual awareness allows us to navigate life's complexities with greater grace and acceptance.

Gratitude as a Daily Practice

Cultivating gratitude is not a passive experience but an active practice, one that requires intention and consistency. A simple but powerful way to begin is by keeping a gratitude journal.

At the end of each day, take a few moments to write down three things you are grateful for. These could be as significant as a major achievement or as simple as the taste of your morning coffee. Over time, this practice trains the mind to seek out and focus on the positive, even in challenging circumstances.

Another approach is to incorporate gratitude into daily routines. For instance, during meals, take a moment to appreciate the effort that went into producing the food—farmers who grew it, workers who transported it, and the person who prepared it. Similarly, during your commute, you might reflect on the infrastructure that enables your journey or the privilege of having a destination to travel to.

Mindful gratitude can also be expressed in relationships. Taking the time to acknowledge and thank those who contribute to your life— whether through words, actions, or simply their presence—strengthens connections and fosters a sense of mutual appreciation. A heartfelt note of thanks, a genuine compliment, or even a smile can have a profound impact on both the giver and the receiver.

The Transformative Power of Gratitude and Impermanence

Gratitude and impermanence are two sides of the same coin, each enriching our experience of the other. By embracing impermanence, we learn to cherish the present moment and appreciate its fleeting beauty. By practicing gratitude, we cultivate a mindset of abundance, resilience, and contentment, even in the face of life's uncertainties.

As we integrate these perspectives into our lives, we begin to see the world through a lens of wonder and appreciation. The ordinary becomes extraordinary, and the burdens we carry grow lighter. Whether through mindfulness, Stoic reflection, or simple acts of thanks, gratitude and impermanence invite us to live more fully, savoring the richness of life in all its complexity.

Overcoming Cognitive Distortions

The human mind is a powerful tool, capable of extraordinary creativity, insight, and resilience.

Yet, it is also prone to errors in thinking—patterns of distortion that can cloud our judgment, fuel negative emotions, and prevent us from seeing reality clearly. Cognitive distortions, as described in modern psychology, are systematic ways in which our thoughts misrepresent the world. These distortions echo themes explored in philosophy, where thinkers like the Stoics and the Buddha grappled with the traps of irrational thinking and self-deception. By recognizing and addressing these mental patterns, we can cultivate a clearer, more balanced perspective on life.

Understanding Cognitive Distortions: The Invisible Obstacles

Cognitive distortions often operate below the surface of awareness, subtly influencing how we interpret events and make decisions. For example, catastrophizing—a tendency to imagine the worst possible outcome—can magnify minor setbacks into seemingly insurmountable problems. A missed deadline at work, viewed through the lens of catastrophizing, might spiral into fears of job loss and personal failure, even when such outcomes are unlikely.

Similarly, black-and-white thinking reduces the complexity of life into rigid categories of all-or-nothing. Success becomes synonymous with perfection, and anything less feels like failure. This kind of thinking often leaves little room for nuance, fostering frustration and discouragement when reality inevitably falls short of impossible standards.

These distortions are not new to human experience. The Stoics, for instance, recognized the tendency of the mind to exaggerate fears and misinterpret reality. Epictetus warned against allowing our judgments to distort our understanding of events, emphasizing that it is not the events themselves that disturb us but the interpretations we attach to them. The Buddha, too, addressed the mind's capacity for illusion, teaching that much of our suffering arises from distorted perceptions and clinging to false beliefs.

The Intersection of Philosophy and Psychol-

ogy

Modern psychology provides tools to identify and challenge cognitive distortions, drawing on insights that parallel ancient philosophical wisdom. Cognitive Behavioral Therapy (CBT), a widely used therapeutic approach, is particularly effective in addressing distorted thinking. At its core, CBT encourages individuals to examine their thoughts critically, asking questions like: Is this thought based on evidence? Am I considering alternative perspectives? How might I view this situation more constructively?

This process aligns with the Socratic Method of questioning, which involves dissecting assumptions and exploring deeper truths. Just as Socrates guided his students to question their beliefs, CBT helps individuals interrogate their automatic thoughts, replacing distorted patterns with more balanced and realistic interpretations.

Consider the example of a person experiencing anxiety about an upcoming presentation. A catastrophic thought might be, "If I make a mistake, everyone will think I'm incompetent." Applying CBT principles, the person could challenge this belief: "Is it true that one mistake will ruin my credibility? Haven't I prepared well and handled similar situations successfully in the past?" This reframing not only reduces anxiety but also fosters a sense of self-efficacy and resilience.

Philosophical Tools for Clarity

Philosophy offers complementary strategies for overcoming cognitive distortions by encouraging a broader and more grounded perspective. Stoicism, with its emphasis on reason and emotional regulation, provides a framework for responding to irrational thoughts. Marcus Aurelius, in his *Meditations*, wrote, "You have power over your mind—not outside events. Realize this, and you will find strength." This principle reminds us that while we cannot control every circumstance, we can control how we think about and respond to those circumstances.

One practical Stoic exercise is the dichotomy of control, which involves distinguishing between what is within our power and what is not. For example, if a colleague criticizes your work, the criticism itself lies outside your control. However, your response—whether you choose to internalize the critique, learn from it, or dismiss it—remains entirely within your sphere of influence. By focusing on what we can change and releasing what we cannot, we reduce the mental strain caused by distorted thinking.

Buddhist mindfulness practices also offer a path to clarity, particularly in dealing with automatic and unhelpful thoughts. Through mindfulness, we learn to observe our thoughts as they arise, recognizing them as transient mental events rather than absolute truths. This practice creates space between stimulus and response, allowing us to choose how we engage with our thoughts. For instance, when a self-critical thought surfaces—"I'm not good enough"—mindfulness invites us to acknowledge it without judgment and let it pass, rather than clinging to it or letting it define our sense of self.

Practical Steps for Reframing Negative Thoughts

Overcoming cognitive distortions is not about suppressing negative thoughts but about transforming our relationship with them. One effective technique is thought journaling, a practice rooted in both CBT and philosophical reflection. By writing down troubling thoughts, identifying their underlying distortions, and reframing them in a more balanced light, we begin to shift habitual patterns of thinking.

For example, if you find yourself catastrophizing about a minor conflict with a friend, your journal entry might look like this:

- **Thought:** "They're probably angry and don't want to talk to me anymore."
- **Distortion:** Jumping to conclusions without evidence.
- **Reframe:** "I don't know how they're feeling right now. It's possible they're busy or preoccupied. I can check in with them to clarify."

Another tool is the use of affirmations rooted in philosophical principles. The Stoic affirmation, "I can endure and overcome," reinforces resilience, while a Buddhist-inspired affirmation, "This moment is temporary," fosters acceptance. By repeating these affirmations during moments of stress, we counteract distorted thinking with constructive truths.

The Path to Clarity and Empowerment

Recognizing and addressing cognitive distortions is a journey of self-awareness and growth. It requires patience and practice, as well as a willingness to confront the habits of mind that no longer serve us. Yet, the rewards are profound: greater emotional balance, improved relationships, and a clearer understanding of ourselves and the world.

By integrating the insights of philosophy and psychology, we gain powerful tools for navigating life's complexities. Whether through Socratic questioning, Stoic reframing, or mindfulness practices, we learn to see beyond the illusions of distorted thinking, uncovering a perspective that is both grounded and liberating. In this clarity, we find not only the strength to face challenges but also the freedom to live with greater authenticity and purpose.

The Growth Mindset – Transforming Challenges

The way we perceive challenges shapes the trajectory of our personal growth. While some see obstacles as insurmountable, others view them as opportunities for learning and improvement. This difference lies at the heart of the growth mindset, a concept developed by psychologist Carol Dweck. Rooted in the belief that abilities and intelligence can be cultivated through effort and persistence, the growth mindset offers a transformative way to approach life's difficulties. When paired with classical ideas of self-improvement from philosophy, it becomes a powerful tool for personal transformation.

Carol Dweck's Growth Mindset: The Power of Belief

Dweck's research contrasts the growth mindset with its counterpart, the fixed mindset. In a fixed mindset, individuals see their abilities as static traits: intelligence, talent, and character are perceived as unchangeable. Failure, in this view, becomes a reflection of inherent limitations rather than a stepping stone to progress.

The growth mindset, by contrast, embraces challenges as opportunities to develop. It reframes failure not as evidence of inadequacy but as an essential part of the learning process.

One of Dweck's most famous studies involved children solving puzzles. Those with a growth mindset persisted through increasingly difficult tasks, seeing the challenges as a chance to stretch their abilities. Children with a fixed mindset, however, gave up more easily, viewing the struggle as a sign of personal failure. This research underscores a profound truth: how we interpret setbacks determines how we respond to them.

For adults, the implications are equally profound. A person with a growth mindset might view a career setback—a missed promotion or a challenging project—as an opportunity to build skills, deepen resilience, and prepare for future success. In contrast, someone with a fixed mindset might internalize the experience as a verdict on their competence, leading to stagnation and self-doubt. Dweck's work reminds us that cultivating a growth mindset is not just about positive thinking but about fostering a deeper belief in our capacity for change.

Classical Ideas of Self-Improvement

The concept of the growth mindset is not new; it resonates with age-old philosophical traditions that emphasize self-improvement through effort and reflection. Aristotle, for instance, believed that excellence is achieved through practice. "We are what we repeatedly do," he wrote. "Excellence, then, is not an act but a habit." This idea parallels the growth mindset's focus on perseverance and the incremental nature of progress. For Aristotle, virtues like courage and wisdom are not innate but cultivated through consistent action and deliberate effort.

The Stoics, too, emphasized the importance of growth through adversity. Seneca wrote that hardship is a training ground for greatness, likening challenges to a whetstone that sharpens the mind and spirit. This perspective reframes difficulties not as barriers but as opportunities to develop inner strength. A Stoic might approach a financial setback not with despair but with determination, asking: What can I learn from this experience? How can I grow stronger as a result?

These classical ideas align with Dweck's work, highlighting a shared belief that growth requires effort, persistence, and an openness to failure. They remind us that transformation is not instantaneous but a gradual process of becoming, one shaped by the choices we make each day.

Embracing Failure as a Teacher

At the heart of the growth mindset is the idea that failure is not the opposite of success but a vital part of it. This perspective challenges cultural narratives that equate success with perfection and failure with defeat. Instead, it invites us to view setbacks as valuable lessons, essential for growth and innovation.

Consider the story of Thomas Edison, who famously said of his attempts to invent the lightbulb, "I have not failed. I've just found 10,000 ways that won't work." Edison's persistence reflects a growth mindset, transforming each setback into a stepping stone toward his ultimate achievement. His example underscores the importance of resilience and curiosity in overcoming obstacles.

In everyday life, embracing failure involves shifting our internal dialogue. Rather than asking, "Why did this happen to me?" we might ask, "What can I learn from this?" This shift fosters a sense of agency and empowerment, transforming moments of struggle into opportunities for self-discovery and improvement.

Practical Steps to Cultivate a Growth Mindset

Developing a growth mindset is not about ignoring challenges but about changing how we engage with them. One effective practice is to reframe negative self-talk. When faced with a difficult task, replace fixed mindset statements like "I'm not good at this" with growth-oriented affirmations such as "I'm not good at this yet, but I can improve with practice." This subtle shift in language reinforces the belief in our capacity for growth.

Another strategy is to seek feedback actively. Constructive criticism, often viewed as a threat to self-esteem, becomes a valuable tool for learning when approached with a growth mindset. By asking for and reflecting on feedback, we gain insights into areas for improvement and refine our approach to challenges.

Setting process-oriented goals, rather than outcome-oriented ones, also aligns with the growth mindset. For example, instead of aiming to "win a promotion," focus on building the skills and relationships that will make the promotion possible. This approach emphasizes effort and progress, reducing the fear of failure while fostering a sense of achievement along the way.

Finally, celebrate progress, no matter how small. Recognizing incremental improvements reinforces the idea that growth is a journey rather than a destination. Whether it's mastering a new skill, overcoming a fear, or navigating a tough conversation, each step forward is a testament to your resilience and commitment.

The Transformative Potential of a Growth Mindset

The growth mindset is more than a tool for personal success; it is a philosophy of living that embraces change, challenges, and the boundless potential for self-improvement. By adopting this perspective, we free ourselves from the constraints of perfectionism and fear, opening the door to creativity, resilience, and fulfillment.

When paired with classical ideas of self-improvement, the growth mindset becomes a bridge between ancient wisdom and modern life. It reminds us that the path to transformation is not linear but iterative, marked by effort, reflection, and the willingness to try again. In the words of the Buddha, "No matter how hard the past, you can always begin again."

As we cultivate this mindset, we not only transform how we view challenges but also how we view ourselves. We begin to see failure not as a limitation but as an invitation to grow. In doing so, we unlock the potential to live more fully, embracing the journey of becoming with courage and grace.

CHAPTER 3: THE ART OF BALANCE – NAVIGATING A BUSY LIFE

Philosophical Foundations of Balance

Balance is a universal principle, present in every facet of life—from the rhythms of nature to the choices we make daily. It is both a guiding ideal and a practical necessity, offering a path to harmony in a world that often pulls us in conflicting directions. Across cultures and centuries, philosophers have explored the art of balance, emphasizing its role in cultivating a fulfilling and meaningful life. From the Taoist principle of Yin-Yang to Aristotle's "Golden Mean," these timeless teachings provide invaluable insights for navigating modern challenges, such as work-life imbalance and the constant demands of a busy life.

The Taoist Principle of Yin-Yang

In Taoist philosophy, balance is symbolized by the principle of Yin-Yang—a dynamic interplay between opposing forces that, when in harmony, create wholeness. Yin represents qualities such as stillness, receptivity, and intuition, while Yang embodies action, assertiveness, and logic. Neither is inherently good or bad; rather, their coexistence and interdependence sustain the flow of life. The famous Yin-Yang symbol, with its swirling black and white halves, reminds us that balance is not static but fluid—a dynamic process of adaptation.

This principle holds profound relevance in today's fast-paced world. Consider the modern dilemma of work-life balance. Many individuals, driven by the demands of career ambition (Yang), neglect the restorative aspects of life, such as leisure, relationships, and self-care (Yin). The result is often burnout, dissatisfaction, and a sense of disconnection. Taoist wisdom suggests that true balance arises not from rigidly dividing our time but from recognizing and honoring the interplay between these forces. Just as night follows day and rest follows activity, a harmonious life requires periods of both striving and stillness.

Applying the Yin-Yang principle might involve integrating moments of quiet reflection into a busy schedule, allowing intuition and creativity to complement logical problem-solving. For example, a professional facing a difficult decision could benefit from stepping away to meditate or take a walk, creating space for insights to emerge naturally. This approach aligns with the Taoist belief that balance is not achieved by forcing outcomes but by flowing with the natural rhythms of life.

Aristotle's "Golden Mean"

While Taoism focuses on the interplay of opposites, Aristotle's concept of the "Golden Mean" emphasizes moderation as the path to virtue. In his *Nicomachean Ethics*, Aristotle argued that every virtue lies between two extremes—excess and deficiency. Courage, for example, is the mean between recklessness and cowardice, while generosity lies between extravagance and stinginess. For Aristotle, living well requires navigating these extremes with wisdom, cultivating habits that promote balance and harmony.

The Golden Mean resonates deeply with modern challenges, where excess often masquerades as success. Overworking, overcommitting, or overindulging can lead to imbalance, just as underperforming or withdrawing can result in missed opportunities. Aristotle's framework encourages us to examine our actions and attitudes, seeking the middle ground that aligns with our values and goals.

For instance, in managing a demanding workload, the Golden Mean might involve setting boundaries that prioritize both productivity and well-being. This could mean saying no to unnecessary meetings, delegating tasks, or scheduling time for rest and recreation. By practicing moderation, we create a sustainable rhythm that supports long-term success rather than short-term exhaustion.

Balance in Nature and Human Experience

The natural world offers countless examples of balance, reinforcing its importance as a universal principle. Seasons transition seamlessly, ecosystems thrive through equilibrium, and the human body functions optimally when its systems are in harmony. These patterns remind us that balance is not a rigid state but a dynamic process of adjustment and recalibration.

In human experience, this dynamic nature is evident in the way we navigate relationships, responsibilities, and personal growth. A parent balancing career and family life, for example, must continuously adapt to shifting priorities, recognizing that balance is not about perfection but about presence. Similarly, an artist striving to balance creative freedom with financial stability learns to embrace the tension between these forces, finding inspiration in their interplay.

The philosopher Confucius captured this idea beautifully when he said, "Balance is the greatest of virtues, for it unites all others." His teachings emphasize the importance of harmony in personal conduct and social interactions, reminding us that balance extends beyond individual well-being to encompass our relationships and contributions to the broader community.

Modern Applications of Ancient Wisdom

The philosophical foundations of balance offer practical guidance for addressing the complexities of modern life. One key insight is the importance of mindfulness—cultivating awareness of when we are veering toward excess or deficiency and making intentional adjustments. For example, if we notice that work is consuming our evenings, we might set a firm boundary to disconnect and spend quality time with loved ones. Conversely, if we find ourselves procrastinating, we can gently steer our energy toward productive action.

Another practical application is the practice of self-reflection. By regularly evaluating our priorities and habits, we gain clarity about where imbalance may be occurring and how to restore equilibrium. Journaling, for instance, can help us identify patterns of overcommitment or neglect, allowing us to make conscious choices that align with our values.

Finally, embracing the fluid nature of balance means cultivating flexibility and resilience. Life is inherently unpredictable, and even the best-laid plans can be disrupted. Rather than striving for a fixed ideal of balance, we can adopt a mindset of adaptability, flowing with change while maintaining a clear sense of purpose. This approach echoes both Taoist and Aristotelian wisdom, reminding us that balance is not a destination but an ongoing journey.

The Timeless Pursuit of Harmony

At its heart, the art of balance is a practice of alignment—bringing our actions, priorities, and values into harmony. The teachings of Taoism and Aristotle provide a rich foundation for understanding this principle, offering timeless wisdom that resonates across cultures and contexts. In a world that often feels overwhelming, their insights remind us that balance is both attainable and essential, a path to greater fulfillment, resilience, and meaning.

As we navigate the demands of modern life, we can draw on these philosophical foundations to guide our choices and actions. By honoring the interplay of Yin and Yang, seeking the Golden Mean, and embracing the dynamic nature of balance, we cultivate a life that is not only productive but also joyful and deeply connected. This pursuit, though challenging, is among the most rewarding of all, offering a sense of wholeness that transcends the chaos of the everyday.

Practical Strategies for Prioritization

In an age of relentless demands and competing priorities, the ability to effectively manage our time and energy has become essential. Without a clear sense of direction, we risk becoming overwhelmed by tasks that feel urgent but lack true importance. Prioritization is the antidote to this chaos, enabling us to align our actions with our goals and values. By setting boundaries and focusing on what truly matters, we can create space for balance and fulfillment in our lives.

Philosophy and modern productivity techniques offer invaluable guidance for this endeavor. From Aristotle's reflections on purposeful action to the practical insights of the Eisenhower Matrix, these tools provide both timeless wisdom and actionable strategies for navigating the complexities of a busy life.

The Philosophy of Purposeful Action

At the heart of effective prioritization lies the principle of intentionality. Aristotle emphasized that meaningful action requires a clear understanding of our ultimate goals. He argued that every choice should be directed toward what he called *eudaimonia*—a state of flourishing and fulfillment. This perspective encourages us to evaluate our tasks not simply by their immediate demands but by their alignment with our broader aspirations.

For example, consider a professional faced with the decision of whether to take on an additional project. Through Aristotle's lens, the question becomes not just "Can I do this?" but "Does this contribute to my long-term growth and well-being?" This shift in perspective helps us distinguish between activities that are truly valuable and those that merely consume our time and energy.

Modern prioritization techniques build on this philosophical foundation, translating abstract ideals into practical steps. By combining the clarity of purpose advocated by Aristotle with structured frameworks, we can make more intentional choices in our daily lives.

The Eisenhower Matrix: Urgency vs. Impor-

tance

One of the most effective tools for prioritization is the Eisenhower Matrix, named after U.S. President Dwight D. Eisenhower, who famously said, "What is important is seldom urgent, and what is urgent is seldom important." This method categorizes tasks into four quadrants based on their urgency and importance:

1. **Urgent and Important:** Tasks that require immediate attention and have significant consequences, such as meeting a deadline or addressing a crisis.

2. **Important but Not Urgent:** Activities that contribute to long-term goals, such as planning, learning, or building relationships.

3. **Urgent but Not Important:** Tasks that demand attention but do not align with our priorities, such as answering trivial emails or attending unnecessary meetings.

4. **Neither Urgent Nor Important:** Distractions that add little value, such as excessive scrolling

on social media or procrastination.

By using the Eisenhower Matrix, we can allocate our time more effectively, focusing on activities in the first two quadrants while minimizing or delegating those in the latter two. This approach not only enhances productivity but also reduces stress, as we gain a clearer sense of what truly deserves our attention.

The Art of Saying No

An essential skill for prioritization is the ability to set boundaries and say no. While it can be tempting to accommodate every request or opportunity, doing so often leads to overcommitment and burnout. Learning to decline tasks that do not align with our priorities is not an act of selfishness but a way of preserving our energy for what matters most.

Philosopher Seneca, a prominent Stoic, wrote about the importance of valuing our time. In his essay *On the Shortness of Life*, he observed that many people squander their days on trivial pursuits, only to lament the lack of time for what truly matters. His advice is as relevant today as it was in ancient Rome: "It is not that we have a short time to live, but that we waste much of it."

In practice, saying no involves both clarity and tact. For example, when faced with a request that conflicts with your priorities, you might respond by expressing appreciation for the opportunity but explaining your current commitments. This approach allows you to uphold your boundaries while maintaining positive relationships.

Time-Blocking and Focus

Another practical strategy for prioritization is time-blocking—a method of scheduling specific blocks of time for different tasks. By allocating dedicated periods for work, rest, and personal growth, we create a structured rhythm that supports balance. Time-blocking not only enhances focus but also prevents the constant interruptions that often derail our progress.

Consider a writer working on a book. By designating mornings for creative writing and afternoons for administrative tasks, they can fully immerse themselves in each activity without the distraction of competing demands. This approach mirrors the ancient practice of setting aside sacred time for reflection and learning, a tradition upheld by many great thinkers.

Time-blocking also fosters mindfulness, as it encourages us to be fully present in each moment. Rather than multitasking or rushing from one activity to the next, we approach each task with intention and care, embodying the principles of balance in our daily lives.

The Role of Reflection in Prioritization

Effective prioritization is not a one-time decision but an ongoing process of evaluation and adjustment. Just as a sailor continually adjusts their course to stay aligned with their destination, we must regularly reflect on our choices to ensure they remain consistent with our values and goals.

Journaling is a powerful tool for this purpose. By taking a few minutes each day or week to review our actions, we gain insight into what is working, what is not, and where adjustments are needed. For example, a journal entry might reveal that too much time is being spent on urgent but unimportant tasks, prompting a shift in focus toward long-term priorities.

Reflection also allows us to celebrate progress and acknowledge the small victories that often go unnoticed. This practice reinforces a sense of accomplishment and motivates us to continue striving for balance and fulfillment.

Prioritization as a Path to Freedom

At its core, prioritization is about reclaiming our time and energy from the chaos of modern life. It empowers us to make intentional choices, aligning our actions with our deepest values and aspirations. Whether through the clarity of Aristotle's purposeful action, the structure of the Eisenhower Matrix, or the discipline of time-blocking, prioritization offers a path to freedom—freedom from overwhelm, distraction, and regret.

By embracing these strategies, we create space for what truly matters, cultivating a life that is not only productive but also meaningful and balanced. In doing so, we honor the timeless wisdom of those who came before us, applying their insights to the unique challenges of our time. Prioritization, like balance itself, is both an art and a practice—one that holds the key to navigating a busy life with grace and intention.

The Role of Rest and Renewal

In the pursuit of balance, rest and renewal are not indulgences but necessities. Just as nature has its seasons of growth and dormancy, so too must we alternate between action and recovery to maintain harmony in our lives. Yet, in a culture that often equates busyness with productivity, the value of rest is frequently overlooked. The wisdom of ancient traditions and modern science reminds us that rest is not a retreat from life's demands but a vital part of meeting them with clarity, resilience, and creativity.

Ancient Traditions: The Rhythm of Renewal

Throughout history, cultures have recognized the importance of rest as an integral part of life's rhythm. In Taoism, the concept of *wu wei*, often translated as "effortless action," emphasizes the value of aligning with the natural flow rather than pushing against it. This philosophy suggests that periods of rest are not wasted time but essential for maintaining balance and harmony. Just as a river's stillness creates the conditions for its powerful flow, rest replenishes the energy needed for purposeful action.

Similarly, the Sabbath, a day of rest observed in many religious traditions, embodies the principle of renewal. In Judaism, the Sabbath is considered a time to step away from work and reconnect with one's faith, family, and inner self. This practice reflects the understanding that rest is not only restorative but also sacred—a means of honoring the rhythms of life.

These ancient practices serve as powerful reminders that rest is not the opposite of productivity but its foundation. By creating intentional pauses in our routines, we cultivate the energy and focus needed to engage fully with the tasks and challenges before us.

Modern Science: The Physiology of Rest

Modern science offers compelling evidence for the importance of rest in sustaining physical and mental well-being. Sleep, for instance, is not merely a passive state but an active process during which the brain consolidates memories, repairs tissues, and regulates emotions. Chronic sleep deprivation has been linked to a host of negative outcomes, including impaired decision-making, reduced creativity, and heightened stress.

Equally important is the role of "active rest," or deliberate activities that promote relaxation and rejuvenation. Practices such as yoga, meditation, and even leisurely walks have been shown to reduce cortisol levels, enhance focus, and improve overall health. These activities align with the principles of mindfulness, encouraging us to slow down and reconnect with the present moment.

One particularly intriguing concept is the ultradian rhythm—a natural cycle of energy and focus that occurs throughout the day. Research suggests that our ability to concentrate peaks in 90-minute intervals, followed by periods of lower energy. Ignoring these natural cycles, as many of us do in the name of productivity, often leads to diminishing returns. By incorporating short breaks into our schedules, we honor these rhythms, enhancing both performance and well-being.

The Role of Reflection in Renewal

Rest is not only physical but also mental and emotional. Reflection, a form of cognitive rest, allows us to process experiences, gain insights, and reset our perspective. The philosopher Seneca emphasized the importance of reflection in his writings, describing it as a nightly ritual of reviewing the day's events and assessing his actions. This practice, he believed, fostered self-awareness and prepared him to face each new day with clarity and purpose.

In modern life, reflection often takes the form of journaling, meditation, or simply setting aside time to think without distraction. These practices help us step back from the noise of daily life, offering a broader perspective on our goals, challenges, and achievements. For example, after a stressful week at work, a reflective journaling session might reveal patterns of over-commitment or areas where boundaries could be strengthened. This kind of insight transforms rest into a tool for growth, enabling us to navigate life's demands more effectively.

The Cost of Neglecting Rest

When rest is neglected, the consequences ripple through every aspect of our lives. Physically, prolonged periods of stress and overexertion can lead to burnout, fatigue, and chronic health conditions. Mentally, the lack of rest impairs our ability to think clearly, solve problems, and manage emotions. Even our relationships suffer, as irritability and exhaustion erode the patience and presence needed to connect with others.

The paradox of rest is that it often feels unproductive in the moment, yet it is one of the most effective ways to enhance long-term productivity. Consider the example of a marathon runner who trains without adequate recovery. While their initial performance might improve, the cumulative strain eventually leads to injury and diminished results. The same principle applies to all areas of life: without rest, we risk depleting the very resources that sustain our success.

Creating Space for Rest and Renewal

Incorporating rest into a busy life requires intentionality and commitment. One effective approach is to schedule rest just as you would any other priority. For instance, setting aside a specific time each evening to unwind—whether through reading, meditation, or a hobby—creates a structured opportunity for renewal. Similarly, taking regular vacations or even short weekend retreats provides a chance to step away from daily demands and recharge.

Another strategy is to establish rituals that signal the transition from activity to rest. This might include turning off electronic devices an hour before bed, lighting a candle to create a calming atmosphere, or practicing deep breathing exercises to release tension. These rituals not only enhance the quality of rest but also cultivate a sense of mindfulness and intention.

Finally, embracing rest as a mindset involves letting go of guilt or resistance. In a culture that glorifies busyness, rest can feel like an act of defiance—a deliberate choice to prioritize well-being over relentless productivity. By re-framing rest as an investment in our health, relationships, and creativity, we honor its essential role in a balanced and fulfilling life.

The Transformative Power of Rest

Rest and renewal are not luxuries but vital components of a balanced life. They provide the space for reflection, creativity, and growth, enabling us to engage with the world from a place of strength and clarity. The wisdom of ancient traditions, combined with modern scientific insights, reminds us that rest is not a pause from life's demands but a means of meeting them more fully.

As we navigate the complexities of a busy life, the art of rest invites us to slow down, listen to our inner rhythms, and reconnect with what truly matters. Whether through sleep, active rest, or moments of quiet reflection, rest empowers us to live with greater purpose, resilience, and joy. In embracing this essential practice, we create a foundation for balance that sustains us not only in the present but throughout the journey of life.

Integrating Balance into Everyday Living

Balance is not a destination but a practice—a dynamic process of aligning our actions with our values while navigating the complexities of life. The demands of work, relationships, and personal growth often pull us in different directions, but with intention and effort, balance can become a natural rhythm rather than a fleeting goal. By embedding practices of mindfulness, routine evaluation, and flexibility into daily life, we create a foundation for sustained harmony and fulfillment.

Mindfulness: Anchoring in the Present

Mindfulness lies at the heart of balance, inviting us to engage fully with the present moment rather than being overwhelmed by past regrets or future anxieties. Rooted in Buddhist traditions and embraced by modern psychology, mindfulness cultivates awareness of our thoughts, emotions, and surroundings. This practice fosters clarity and intentionality, helping us respond to life's demands with composure and purpose.

Imagine a busy professional juggling deadlines and family responsibilities. Without mindfulness, their attention might be scattered, leading to mistakes at work and strained interactions at home. Mindfulness, however, encourages a different approach: pausing to take a few deep breaths before transitioning from one task to another, fully focusing on the task at hand, and engaging with loved ones without distractions. These small but significant moments of presence transform a chaotic day into one marked by connection and purpose.

Incorporating mindfulness into daily routines does not require dramatic changes. It might involve beginning the morning with a moment of gratitude, pausing to notice the sensation of water while washing dishes, or ending the day with a brief meditation. These practices ground us in the present, reducing stress and enhancing our ability to maintain balance.

Routine Evaluation: Adjusting the Compass

Even with the best intentions, maintaining balance requires regular reflection and adjustment. Life is dynamic, and what worked yesterday may no longer serve us today. Routine evaluation acts as a compass, guiding us back to our priorities when we veer off course.

The philosopher Socrates emphasized the importance of self-examination, famously declaring, "The unexamined life is not worth living." In modern terms, this might mean setting aside time each week or month to assess how well our actions align with our values and goals. Are we spending too much time on urgent but unimportant tasks? Are we neglecting areas of life that bring us joy and fulfillment? Honest reflection allows us to identify imbalances and make intentional changes.

A practical tool for this process is journaling. By writing about our experiences, successes, and challenges, we gain insight into patterns and areas for improvement. For example, a journal entry might reveal that time spent on social media has increased while time with loved ones has decreased, prompting a conscious decision to shift priorities. Routine evaluation ensures that balance remains a living, adaptable practice rather than a static ideal.

Flexibility: Embracing Change with Grace

Flexibility is another cornerstone of balance, allowing us to adapt to life's inevitable shifts without losing our center. The Taoist principle of *wu wei*, or effortless action, teaches that resistance to change creates tension, while flowing with change fosters harmony. Flexibility does not mean abandoning our goals or values but approaching challenges with openness and creativity.

Consider a parent whose child unexpectedly falls ill on a day packed with meetings. A rigid mindset might lead to frustration and guilt, while a flexible mindset reframes the situation as an opportunity to prioritize caregiving and reschedule tasks. Flexibility empowers us to respond to the unexpected with resilience, maintaining balance even in the face of disruption.

One way to cultivate flexibility is by adopting a "both/and" mindset. Instead of viewing situations as either/or—success or failure, work or rest—we embrace the possibility of integrating multiple priorities. For instance, a professional who values both career advancement and family time might explore flexible work arrangements or involve family in aspects of their work. This approach reflects the fluidity of balance, where seemingly competing demands can coexist harmoniously.

Creating Rituals for Balance

Rituals provide structure and intention, anchoring balance in daily life. These rituals do not need to be elaborate; their power lies in their consistency and meaning. For example, a morning ritual might involve stretching, journaling, and setting an intention for the day, while an evening ritual could include reflection, gratitude, and disconnecting from electronic devices.

Rituals also foster a sense of rhythm, reinforcing the balance between action and rest. A weekly family dinner, a monthly personal retreat, or a yearly vacation becomes a sacred pause, a moment to reconnect with what matters most. These rituals act as touchstones, reminding us to prioritize our well-being amidst life's busyness.

Building a Supportive Environment

Balance is not achieved in isolation; it is shaped by the environments we inhabit and the people we surround ourselves with. Creating a supportive environment involves both physical and relational elements. On a physical level, this might mean decluttering our workspace to reduce distractions or designing a home that fosters relaxation and connection.

On a relational level, building a network of supportive individuals—friends, family, mentors— provides a foundation of encouragement and accountability. Sharing our goals and challenges with others not only deepens our relationships but also reinforces our commitment to balance. For example, discussing a work-life boundary with a partner ensures mutual understanding and support, making it easier to uphold.

The Continuous Journey of Balance

Integrating balance into everyday living is not a one-size-fits-all process but a deeply personal journey. It requires experimentation, reflection, and a willingness to adapt as circumstances evolve. Some days will feel balanced and harmonious, while others may feel chaotic and disjointed. The key is to approach this journey with patience and compassion, recognizing that balance is not about perfection but about progress.

As we cultivate mindfulness, evaluate our routines, embrace flexibility, and create supportive environments, we move closer to a life that reflects our deepest values. This journey is not without its challenges, but it is also rich with rewards: greater clarity, resilience, and a profound sense of fulfillment.

The art of balance invites us to live with intention, embracing both the complexities and the joys of modern life. By integrating these practices into our daily routines, we create a life that is not only productive but also deeply meaningful—a life in which we can truly thrive.

CHAPTER 4: BUILDING RESILIENCE – THRIVING THROUGH ADVERSITY

Resilience in Philosophy and History

Resilience—the ability to endure hardship and emerge stronger—has long been a cornerstone of human existence. In moments of adversity, it is resilience that allows individuals to adapt, persevere, and find meaning in even the harshest circumstances. Philosophers and historical figures throughout time have explored this concept, offering profound insights into how we can cultivate inner strength and thrive through life's inevitable challenges.

From Friedrich Nietzsche's bold assertion that "What doesn't kill me makes me stronger" to Viktor Frankl's reflections on finding purpose in suffering, these teachings illuminate a timeless truth: resilience is not about avoiding pain but about navigating it with courage and intention. Their wisdom, rooted in both thought and action, provides a framework for understanding and building resilience in our own lives.

Nietzsche: Strength Through Struggle

Friedrich Nietzsche, the provocative German philosopher, was no stranger to adversity.

Plagued by illness and isolation for much of his life, Nietzsche developed a philosophy that celebrated struggle as a path to strength and self-realization. His declaration, "What doesn't kill me makes me stronger," encapsulates his belief that hardship, rather than diminishing us, has the potential to elevate us.

For Nietzsche, resilience was not a passive state but an active engagement with life's challenges. He saw suffering as an integral part of growth, urging individuals to embrace discomfort as a necessary step toward achieving their fullest potential. This idea is evident in his concept of the *Übermensch* (Overman), a figure who transcends ordinary existence by overcoming obstacles and affirming life's inherent difficulties.

Imagine someone facing the loss of a job. Through a Nietzschean lens, this setback could be seen not as a defeat but as an opportunity to reassess priorities, develop new skills, and pursue a more fulfilling path. Nietzsche challenges us to reframe adversity as a crucible for transformation, where resilience is forged through effort and perseverance.

Viktor Frankl: Meaning in Suffering

While Nietzsche celebrated the strengthening power of struggle, Viktor Frankl brought a deeply human perspective to resilience. A Holocaust survivor and psychiatrist, Frankl endured unimaginable suffering in Nazi concentration camps, losing his family and enduring physical and emotional torment. Yet, in the face of such profound hardship, Frankl discovered a profound truth: even in the darkest moments, we have the capacity to find meaning.

In his seminal work, *Man's Search for Meaning*, Frankl argues that resilience arises from a sense of purpose. He observed that those who survived the camps were often those who could connect their suffering to something greater— whether a commitment to loved ones, a sense of duty, or a belief in a higher cause. Frankl's philosophy, known as logotherapy, emphasizes the power of purpose in fostering resilience.

For modern readers, Frankl's insights offer a powerful reminder that meaning is not something we passively receive but something we actively create. A parent caring for a sick child might find resilience in their commitment to providing comfort, while an entrepreneur facing setbacks might draw strength from their vision of creating something meaningful. By anchoring ourselves in purpose, we cultivate the inner fortitude to endure and thrive.

Resilience in Historical Figures

The lives of historical figures provide vivid examples of resilience in action. Consider Harriet Tubman, who escaped slavery and went on to lead hundreds to freedom via the Underground Railroad. Despite immense physical danger and emotional strain, Tubman's unwavering belief in justice and her determination to liberate others sustained her through her perilous mission. Her story exemplifies the power of resilience rooted in conviction and courage.

Another example is Abraham Lincoln, who faced repeated failures and personal losses before becoming one of America's most revered presidents. From business setbacks to political defeats and the death of his son, Lincoln's life was marked by hardship. Yet, his ability to persevere and maintain his vision for a united nation underscores the importance of resilience in leadership. Lincoln's capacity to learn from failure and remain steadfast in the face of adversity is a testament to the transformative power of resilience.

These stories remind us that resilience is not the absence of difficulty but the ability to confront and grow through it. By studying the lives of those who have endured and triumphed, we gain both inspiration and practical lessons for our own journeys.

Philosophical Lessons on Enduring Hardship

Philosophical teachings further illuminate the path to resilience, offering timeless guidance on enduring and transcending adversity. The Stoics, for instance, emphasized the importance of focusing on what lies within our control. Epictetus, a former slave turned philosopher, advised, "It's not what happens to you, but how you react to it that matters." This perspective encourages us to shift our attention from external events to our internal responses, cultivating resilience through mindset and attitude.

In Buddhism, the concept of *dukkha*—often translated as suffering—acknowledges that pain is an inherent part of existence. However, the Buddha taught that by accepting this reality and practicing mindfulness, we can develop a sense of equanimity that allows us to navigate life's challenges with grace. This approach aligns with modern psychological practices, such as cognitive reframing, which help individuals recontextualize adversity and find growth in hardship.

Both Stoicism and Buddhism remind us that resilience is not about suppressing or denying pain but about engaging with it thoughtfully and constructively. By accepting the inevitability of challenges, we free ourselves from the paralysis of resistance and open the door to transformation.

Applying These Lessons to Modern Life

The wisdom of Nietzsche, Frankl, and other philosophical and historical figures offers a roadmap for building resilience in the face of modern challenges. Whether dealing with personal loss, professional setbacks, or societal upheaval, we can draw on their insights to navigate adversity with strength and purpose.

For example, a student struggling with academic pressure might find solace in Frankl's emphasis on meaning, framing their studies as a step toward a larger goal. A professional facing career uncertainty might adopt a Stoic mindset, focusing on what they can control—such as improving their skills or exploring new opportunities—while accepting what lies beyond their influence.

Resilience, at its core, is a practice. It requires intentional effort, a willingness to confront discomfort, and a commitment to growth. By embracing the lessons of those who have come before us, we can cultivate the inner strength to face life's challenges and emerge not just unbroken but stronger and more fulfilled.

Strengthening the Mind and Spirit

Resilience is not merely an innate quality but a skill that can be cultivated through deliberate practice and reflection. At its core, building resilience involves fortifying the mind and spirit—developing the mental toughness to endure challenges and the emotional resilience to navigate setbacks with grace. Drawing inspiration from Stoicism and Eastern meditative traditions, we discover practical techniques that foster self-discipline, self-compassion, and inner strength.

Stoicism: Mastering the Inner Fortress

The Stoics viewed resilience as a function of mental fortitude, a quality that enables individuals to face life's hardships without succumbing to despair. Central to their philosophy is the concept of control: understanding what lies within our power and what does not. Epictetus, a Stoic philosopher and former slave, taught that while we cannot control external events, we can control our thoughts, emotions, and actions. This realization forms the foundation of mental toughness.

One technique derived from Stoicism is the practice of *negative visualization,* or *premeditatio malorum.* This involves imagining potential challenges or losses in advance, not to dwell on negativity but to prepare the mind for adversity. For instance, before delivering an important presentation, a Stoic might reflect on possible setbacks—technical issues, challenging questions, or a skeptical audience. By envisioning these scenarios, they reduce the fear of the unknown and cultivate a sense of readiness.

Another Stoic practice is cultivating equanimity, or emotional balance, in the face of adversity. Marcus Aurelius, the Roman emperor and Stoic philosopher, often reminded himself that setbacks were a natural part of life. "You have power over your mind—not outside events," he wrote in his *Meditations*. "Realize this, and you will find strength." This mindset fosters resilience by helping us focus on what we can influence, rather than being overwhelmed by circumstances beyond our control.

Eastern Traditions: The Calm Within the Storm

Eastern meditative practices, particularly those rooted in Buddhism, offer complementary techniques for strengthening the mind and spirit. Central to these traditions is the cultivation of mindfulness—the ability to observe thoughts and emotions without becoming entangled in them. Mindfulness trains us to respond to adversity with clarity and intention rather than reacting impulsively.

One powerful practice is *vipassana* meditation, a form of mindfulness that involves observing the impermanent nature of sensations and emotions. By recognizing that even the most intense discomfort will eventually pass, practitioners develop a sense of detachment and resilience. This perspective aligns with the Buddhist teaching of *dukkha*, or suffering, which emphasizes that while pain is inevitable, our relationship to it determines the extent of our suffering.

Consider someone navigating a stressful workplace conflict. Mindfulness might involve taking a few deep breaths, acknowledging the frustration without judgment, and choosing a calm, constructive response. This practice not only diffuses tension but also reinforces the individual's capacity to remain centered amid chaos.

Eastern traditions also emphasize the importance of *metta*, or loving-kindness, toward oneself and others. This practice fosters self-compassion, a crucial component of emotional resilience. In moments of failure or disappointment, self-compassion encourages us to treat ourselves with the same kindness and understanding we would offer a friend. By embracing imperfection and acknowledging our shared humanity, we build the emotional foundation needed to persevere.

The Role of Self-Discipline in Resilience

Self-discipline is the bridge between intention and action—a vital quality for cultivating resilience. Both Stoicism and Eastern practices highlight the importance of daily habits and rituals in strengthening the mind and spirit. These practices create a sense of structure and purpose, grounding us even in uncertain times.

One example is the Stoic principle of "morning and evening reflection." At the start of the day, practitioners set intentions, identifying opportunities to embody virtues such as courage, patience, or wisdom. In the evening, they reflect on their actions, acknowledging successes and learning from mistakes. This ritual fosters self-awareness and accountability, essential for developing resilience.

Similarly, Eastern traditions emphasize the value of consistent practice, whether through meditation, yoga, or mindful breathing. These rituals train the mind to remain present and focused, enhancing our ability to respond effectively to challenges. Over time, the discipline of showing up—even on difficult days—builds a reservoir of inner strength.

Self-discipline also involves setting boundaries to protect our mental and emotional well-being. This might mean saying no to unnecessary commitments, prioritizing rest, or seeking support when needed. Far from being a sign of weakness, these boundaries reflect a deep commitment to resilience, ensuring that we have the capacity to face life's demands with integrity and energy.

The Harmony of Self-Discipline and Self-Compassion

While self-discipline is crucial, it must be balanced with self-compassion to sustain resilience over the long term. Too often, the pursuit of toughness can lead to rigidity or burnout. Self-compassion acts as a counterbalance, reminding us to honor our limitations and embrace moments of rest and renewal.

This harmony is evident in the concept of *yin* and *yang* from Taoist philosophy, which emphasizes the interplay of opposing forces. Just as strength is complemented by softness, discipline must be tempered with kindness. A resilient individual understands when to push forward and when to step back, recognizing that both are necessary for growth.

For example, a marathon runner training for a race must maintain a disciplined regimen of running and conditioning. However, they must also listen to their body, taking rest days to recover and prevent injury. Similarly, in our own lives, resilience involves knowing when to persevere and when to pause, allowing us to navigate challenges with wisdom and grace.

Building a Resilient Mindset

Strengthening the mind and spirit is not a one-time effort but an ongoing journey. It requires patience, practice, and a willingness to learn from both successes and setbacks. By integrating techniques from Stoicism and Eastern traditions, we cultivate the mental and emotional resources needed to thrive through adversity.

This process begins with small, intentional actions: a few minutes of mindfulness each morning, a moment of reflection at day's end, or a conscious effort to reframe negative thoughts. Over time, these practices build a foundation of resilience that supports us through life's uncertainties.

Ultimately, resilience is about more than enduring hardship—it is about emerging stronger, wiser, and more compassionate. By strengthening the mind and spirit, we not only navigate challenges with courage but also create a life imbued with meaning, connection, and purpose. In doing so, we embody the timeless wisdom of those who came before us, carrying their teachings forward into our own journeys.

The Transformative Power of Adversity

Adversity is an inevitable part of life, but within every challenge lies the potential for profound growth and transformation. While pain and hardship can feel overwhelming, they also serve as catalysts for resilience, strength, and self-discovery. This transformative power of adversity is a recurring theme in philosophy, history, and art, offering a framework for navigating difficulties with courage and purpose. By embracing struggle as an opportunity for growth, we unlock the ability to thrive even in the face of life's greatest challenges.

Nietzsche's Philosophy: Growth Through Struggle

Friedrich Nietzsche believed that adversity is not only unavoidable but essential for personal development. His famous assertion, "What doesn't kill me makes me stronger," reflects a deep conviction that struggle is the forge in which strength and character are shaped. For Nietzsche, hardship is not an obstacle to overcome but a necessary step in the journey toward self-actualization.

This philosophy is embodied in his concept of *amor fati*—the love of one's fate. Nietzsche urged individuals to embrace all aspects of their lives, including pain and failure, as integral to their growth. By reframing adversity as an opportunity to develop resilience and clarity, we transform suffering into a source of power. Nietzsche's ideas challenge us to see difficulty not as a burden but as a teacher, guiding us toward our highest potential.

Consider an entrepreneur who faces repeated setbacks in building a business. Through Nietzsche's lens, these challenges are not signs of inadequacy but opportunities to refine skills, strengthen resolve, and clarify purpose. Each failure becomes a stepping stone toward success, cultivating the grit and tenacity needed to persevere.

Kintsugi: Beauty in Brokenness

The Japanese art of kintsugi, or "golden joinery," offers a powerful metaphor for the transformative potential of adversity. This practice involves repairing broken pottery with lacquer mixed with powdered gold, silver, or platinum. The resulting piece is not only restored but enhanced, with its cracks and imperfections highlighted rather than hidden. Kintsugi reflects the belief that flaws and scars are not to be concealed but celebrated as part of an object's history and beauty.

In life, kintsugi teaches us to view our struggles and failures as integral to our journey. Just as a repaired bowl becomes more valuable because of its golden seams, we too can emerge from hardship stronger, wiser, and more compassionate. This philosophy encourages us to embrace vulnerability and imperfection, recognizing that our experiences of loss and pain shape our unique identities.

For example, someone recovering from a significant personal loss might find meaning in supporting others facing similar challenges. By sharing their story and offering empathy, they transform their pain into a source of connection and healing. Like the golden seams of kintsugi, their scars become symbols of resilience and hope.

Historical Examples of Transformation

History is filled with stories of individuals who turned adversity into triumph, demonstrating the transformative power of struggle. Consider Helen Keller, who lost her sight and hearing at a young age but went on to become a renowned author, activist, and advocate for people with disabilities. Her ability to overcome immense challenges was rooted in her resilience and determination, as well as the support of her teacher, Anne Sullivan. Keller's story reminds us that adversity does not define us—it is our response to it that shapes our legacy.

Another powerful example is Nelson Mandela, who endured 27 years of imprisonment during South Africa's apartheid regime. Despite the profound injustice and suffering he faced, Mandela emerged not with bitterness but with a commitment to reconciliation and justice. His ability to transform personal pain into a source of strength and vision united a divided nation, inspiring millions around the world.

These stories highlight the universal truth that adversity, while painful, can also be a springboard for growth and transformation. They challenge us to reflect on our own struggles and consider how we might channel them into meaningful action.

The Growth Mindset and Post-Traumatic Growth

Modern psychology echoes these philosophical and historical insights, particularly through the concept of post-traumatic growth. This phenomenon describes the positive psychological changes that can occur in the aftermath of adversity, such as greater appreciation for life, stronger relationships, and a deeper sense of purpose. Unlike resilience, which focuses on bouncing back, post-traumatic growth emphasizes transformation—emerging from hardship not just intact but enriched.

One way to foster post-traumatic growth is by adopting a growth mindset, a concept developed by psychologist Carol Dweck. The growth mindset views challenges as opportunities to learn and improve, rather than as insurmountable obstacles. This perspective encourages us to embrace failure as part of the process of growth, reinforcing the belief that our abilities and potential are not fixed but expandable.

For instance, a student struggling with a demanding academic course might initially feel discouraged. However, by reframing the challenge as an opportunity to develop perseverance and problem-solving skills, they build not only knowledge but also confidence in their ability to overcome future difficulties.

Practical Applications: Embracing the Transformative Power of Adversity

While the transformative power of adversity is a profound concept, it is not always easy to embrace in the moment. Practical strategies can help us navigate hardship with intention and grace, paving the way for growth:

1. **Reframe Challenges:** Shift your perspective on adversity, viewing it as an opportunity for learning and growth. Ask questions such as,

"What can this teach me?" or "How might this experience strengthen me?"

2. **Cultivate Gratitude:** Even in difficult times, focusing on what we can be grateful for helps to balance our perspective and maintain hope. Gratitude transforms our mindset, allowing us to see beauty and possibility even in the midst of pain.

3. **Seek Meaning:** Like Viktor Frankl's emphasis on purpose, finding meaning in adversity helps us endure and thrive. Reflect on how your struggles align with your values or contribute to a larger goal.

4. **Embrace Vulnerability:** Sharing your challenges with trusted friends, family, or mentors fosters connection and support. Vulnerability is not a weakness but a sign of strength, allowing others to walk alongside us on our journey.

5. **Honor Your Scars:** Just as kintsugi celebrates the beauty of imperfection, take pride in the ways you have grown and transformed through adversity. Your scars are not flaws but testa-

ments to your resilience and courage.

The Promise of Transformation

Adversity is never easy, but it holds the promise of transformation. By embracing challenges with an open heart and a resilient spirit, we uncover our capacity to grow stronger, wiser, and more compassionate. Whether through Nietzsche's philosophy, the art of kintsugi, or the inspiring stories of historical figures, we are reminded that struggle is not the end of the journey—it is the beginning of a new chapter.

As we navigate our own challenges, let us carry this wisdom forward, finding strength in our scars and purpose in our pain. In doing so, we not only transform ourselves but also inspire others to do the same, creating a ripple effect of resilience and hope that extends far beyond our individual lives.

Tools for Resilience in Modern Life

Resilience, while rooted in timeless wisdom and philosophical insight, is ultimately cultivated through practical action. In the face of modern

challenges, the tools we choose to build resilience can be both deeply personal and universally effective. Practices such as journaling, cognitive reframing, and physical disciplines like
yoga and breathwork empower us to navigate
adversity with strength and clarity. These tools
not only help us endure but also foster a mindset of growth, enabling us to thrive through
life's inevitable ups and downs.

Journaling: Writing as a Path to Clarity

Journaling is one of the most accessible and
transformative tools for building resilience. By
putting thoughts onto paper, we externalize our
emotions, creating a safe space to process challenges and reflect on our experiences. This practice, rooted in the ancient tradition of self-examination, encourages self-awareness and fosters
a sense of agency.

The philosopher Marcus Aurelius, a Stoic emperor of Rome, famously kept a journal that
became *Meditations*, a collection of reflections on
life, virtue, and resilience. Through his writing,
Aurelius confronted the burdens of leadership,
the inevitability of loss, and the complexities

of human nature. His journal was not a public work but a private exercise in grounding himself amid chaos—a testament to the enduring power of reflective writing.

In a modern context, journaling can take many forms. A gratitude journal, for instance, shifts focus from what is lacking to what is abundant, cultivating a positive mindset even in difficult times. Reflective journaling, on the other hand, provides an outlet for exploring fears, challenges, and aspirations, enabling us to identify patterns and reframe struggles as opportunities for growth. Whether structured or free-form, the act of journaling transforms internal turbulence into actionable insights, strengthening our capacity for resilience.

Cognitive Reframing: Shifting Perspective

Our thoughts shape our reality, and cognitive reframing—an essential tool for resilience—empowers us to reinterpret challenges in ways that promote strength and clarity. This technique, central to Cognitive Behavioral Therapy (CBT), involves identifying negative or unhelpful thought patterns and replacing them with more constructive alternatives.

For example, someone who has experienced a professional setback might initially think, "I've failed, and I'll never recover." Through cognitive reframing, this thought might transform into, "This is a temporary setback and an opportunity to learn and grow." This shift not only reduces emotional distress but also fosters a proactive mindset, encouraging action rather than defeat.

Cognitive reframing echoes the wisdom of the Stoics, who emphasized the power of perception. Epictetus famously said, "Men are disturbed not by things, but by the view they take of them." By changing how we interpret events, we regain control over our emotional responses, building resilience from within.

Practicing cognitive reframing can begin with simple questions: "What evidence supports this thought?" "How might I view this situation differently?" "What lesson can I take from this experience?" Over time, this practice becomes a habit, enabling us to navigate challenges with greater flexibility and strength.

Yoga and Breathwork: Anchoring the Body and Mind

Resilience is not solely a mental construct; it is deeply rooted in the body. Physical practices like yoga and breathwork provide powerful tools for cultivating resilience by grounding us in the present moment and strengthening our connection between mind and body.

Yoga, with its emphasis on mindful movement and balance, encourages both physical and emotional resilience. The practice of holding poses teaches patience and perseverance, while the focus on breath fosters calm and clarity. Beyond its physical benefits, yoga serves as a metaphor for resilience itself: just as we stretch and strengthen muscles through practice, we stretch and strengthen our capacity to endure challenges.

Breathwork, a complementary practice, harnesses the power of the breath to regulate emotions and promote well-being. Techniques such as diaphragmatic breathing and box breathing activate the parasympathetic nervous system, reducing stress and enhancing focus. In moments of adversity, the simple act of pausing to take a few deep breaths can interrupt cycles of anxiety and create space for thoughtful action.

Consider a teacher overwhelmed by the demands of a busy classroom. By incorporating breathwork into their routine—perhaps a few moments of deep breathing before entering the room—they create a buffer against stress, enhancing their ability to respond to challenges with patience and clarity. Over time, these practices become anchors, providing stability in even the most turbulent times.

The Role of Community in Resilience

While individual practices are essential, resilience is also strengthened through connection and community. The support of trusted friends, family, and mentors provides a foundation of encouragement and perspective, reminding us that we are not alone in our struggles. Sharing our challenges with others not only lightens the emotional burden but also fosters a sense of belonging and mutual growth.

Community can take many forms, from informal gatherings of friends to structured support groups. In each case, the act of coming together to share experiences and insights reinforces our collective resilience. For example, a group of colleagues navigating a challenging project might hold regular check-ins to share progress, offer support, and celebrate small victories. These moments of connection transform individual challenges into shared opportunities for growth.

Integrating Resilience Tools into Daily Life

The true power of these tools lies in their integration into daily life. Resilience is not built in moments of crisis alone but through consistent practice over time. Just as an athlete trains daily to prepare for competition, we must cultivate resilience through intentional routines and habits.

Start small. A five-minute journaling session in the morning, a single reframed thought during a challenging moment, or a brief yoga practice at the end of the day—each of these actions contributes to a foundation of resilience. Over time, these practices become second nature, creating a reservoir of strength to draw upon when adversity arises.

Importantly, resilience is not about perfection but about persistence. There will be days when the practices feel difficult or when setbacks test our resolve. In these moments, self-compassion becomes a vital tool, reminding us to honor our efforts and begin again.

Resilience as a Lifelong Practice

The journey to resilience is ongoing, a dynamic process of growth and adaptation. By incorporating tools such as journaling, cognitive reframing, yoga, and breathwork into our lives, we create a framework for navigating adversity with strength and purpose. These practices, rooted in both ancient wisdom and modern science, empower us to thrive not despite challenges but because of them.

As we build resilience, we not only transform our own lives but also inspire those around us to do the same. In the face of life's uncertainties, these tools serve as beacons of hope and empowerment, guiding us toward a future marked by courage, clarity, and connection. Resilience, after all, is not a destination but a practice—one that enriches every aspect of our journey.

CHAPTER 5: MEANINGFUL CONNECTIONS – PHILOSOPHY IN RELATIONSHIPS

Philosophical Roots of Relationships

Human connection lies at the heart of a meaningful life. From our closest friendships to our broader societal ties, relationships shape who we are and how we navigate the world. Yet, the essence of these connections goes beyond surface-level interaction; it is rooted in authenticity, engagement, and mutual respect. Philosophers across centuries have explored the nature of relationships, offering profound insights into what it means to connect with others in meaningful ways.

Among these thinkers, Aristotle and Martin Buber stand out for their enduring contributions. Aristotle's exploration of friendship and Buber's concept of "I-Thou" relationships offer timeless frameworks for understanding the depth and complexity of human connection.

Aristotle on Friendship: A Foundation for Virtue

In his *Nicomachean Ethics*, Aristotle identified friendship as one of the highest goods in life, essential for achieving *eudaimonia*—a state of flourishing and fulfillment. He categorized friendships into three types: those based on utility, pleasure, and virtue. While friendships of utility and pleasure are transactional and often fleeting, friendships of virtue are enduring and deeply meaningful. These relationships are grounded in mutual respect and a shared commitment to each other's growth and well-being.

For Aristotle, true friendship is transformative. It not only provides comfort and companionship but also serves as a mirror, reflecting our strengths and weaknesses and inspiring us to become better versions of ourselves. In the company of virtuous friends, we are challenged to cultivate our character, guided by the trust and understanding that underpin such bonds.

Consider the relationship between historical figures such as Mahatma Gandhi and his close associate C.F. Andrews. Their friendship, rooted in shared values and a commitment to justice, exemplifies Aristotle's ideal of virtuous friendship. Andrews supported Gandhi during pivotal moments of his activism, while Gandhi inspired Andrews to deepen his own spiritual and ethical convictions. Together, they embodied the transformative potential of meaningful connection.

In our own lives, Aristotle's insights remind us to seek relationships that nurture growth and authenticity. While casual acquaintances and professional networks have their place, it is the relationships built on trust, empathy, and shared values that sustain us through life's challenges and joys.

Martin Buber and the "I-Thou" Relationship

In the early 20th century, philosopher Martin Buber expanded the understanding of human connection with his seminal work, *I and Thou*. Buber distinguished between two modes of relating: "I-It" and "I-Thou." In "I-It" relationships, we treat others as objects, valuing them for their utility or role in our lives. These interactions, while necessary, lack depth and reciprocity.

In contrast, "I-Thou" relationships are marked by genuine presence and mutual recognition. In these moments, we encounter another person not as a means to an end but as a whole being, engaging with them authentically and without pretense. Buber described this connection as a spiritual encounter, one that transcends individual needs and opens the door to profound understanding.

To illustrate this concept, consider the bond between a teacher and a student when they engage in a moment of shared discovery. In an "I-Thou" relationship, the teacher sees the student not merely as a recipient of knowledge but as a collaborator in the learning process. Likewise, the student sees the teacher not as an authority figure but as a guide. This dynamic fosters a deep and meaningful exchange, enriching both parties.

Buber's philosophy challenges us to examine the quality of our relationships. Are we truly present with others, or are we distracted by our own concerns? Do we see the people in our lives as individuals with unique experiences and perspectives, or do we reduce them to their roles and functions? By striving to cultivate "I-Thou" relationships, we deepen our capacity for empathy, connection, and shared humanity.

Authentic Engagement: The Bridge Between

Philosophy and Practice

The philosophical roots of relationships emphasize the importance of authenticity—a quality
that requires us to be fully present and honest
in our interactions. Authentic engagement involves both vulnerability and courage, as it asks
us to show up as our true selves while creating
space for others to do the same.

One way to practice authenticity is by prioritizing active listening. When we listen with
genuine curiosity and without interruption, we
signal to others that their thoughts and feelings matter. This simple act fosters trust and
connection, laying the groundwork for deeper
relationships. For example, during a difficult
conversation with a friend or partner, active
listening can transform a potential conflict into
an opportunity for mutual understanding.

Another aspect of authentic engagement is
embracing imperfection. Relationships are not
about perfection but about mutual growth and
support. When we allow ourselves to be vulnerable, sharing our fears and struggles, we
invite others to do the same. This vulnerability

strengthens bonds, reminding us that we are not alone in our experiences.

The Intersection of Individuality and Connection

While relationships are inherently collaborative, they also honor individuality. Both Aristotle and Buber recognized that meaningful connections do not require us to lose ourselves in others but rather to bring our full selves to the relationship. This balance between individuality and connection is crucial for maintaining healthy and fulfilling bonds.

In practice, this means respecting boundaries and allowing space for growth. Just as a strong friendship supports personal development, a thriving partnership encourages each person to pursue their passions and aspirations. The tension between togetherness and autonomy enriches the relationship, creating a dynamic interplay of support and independence.

Consider the example of a creative partnership, such as that between composers Leonard Bernstein and Stephen Sondheim. Their collaboration on works like *West Side Story* was marked by mutual respect and a shared vision, yet each retained their unique voice and perspective. This balance allowed them to create something greater than either could achieve alone—a testament to the power of connection that honors individuality.

Building Meaningful Connections Today

In a world increasingly characterized by digital communication and fast-paced interactions, the lessons of Aristotle and Buber are more relevant than ever. Meaningful relationships require time, intention, and presence—qualities that can be challenging to cultivate in an era of constant distractions.

To build deeper connections, we can start by slowing down and prioritizing quality over quantity. Rather than spreading ourselves thin across numerous interactions, we can focus on nurturing a few key relationships. Whether through regular conversations, shared experiences, or acts of kindness, these efforts create the foundation for authentic engagement.

Furthermore, the principles of "I-Thou" relationships and virtuous friendship remind us
that connection is not a passive state but an
active practice. By approaching each interaction
with openness and intention, we transform ordinary moments into opportunities for growth
and connection.

Conclusion

The philosophical roots of relationships remind
us that true connection is both a gift and a responsibility. Through the insights of Aristotle and Buber, we see that meaningful bonds
are built on authenticity, presence, and mutual respect. As we navigate the complexities of
modern life, these timeless principles guide
us toward deeper, more fulfilling connections,
enriching both our own lives and the lives of
those we touch.

Empathy and Emotional Intelligence

Empathy—the ability to understand and share
the feelings of another—is the bedrock of mean-

ingful relationships. It enables us to connect beyond words, bridging differences and fostering a sense of shared humanity. When paired with emotional intelligence, which involves recognizing and managing our own emotions while navigating those of others, empathy becomes a powerful tool for building trust, resolving conflicts, and deepening connections. Philosophical traditions like Confucianism and insights from modern neuroscience illuminate the transformative potential of empathy and its role in cultivating meaningful relationships.

Confucianism: The Heart of Empathy

In Confucian philosophy, empathy is not just a personal virtue but a societal cornerstone. Known as *ren*, or humaneness, this principle emphasizes the importance of cultivating compassion and understanding in all interactions. Confucius described *ren* as the essence of ethical behavior, urging individuals to consider the impact of their actions on others. He famously advised, "Do not impose on others what you do not wish for yourself," encapsulating the empathetic ideal of putting oneself in another's shoes.

For Confucius, empathy begins with self-cultivation. By reflecting on our own thoughts and
emotions, we develop the awareness needed
to understand those of others. This process
is not about pity or condescension but about
recognizing our shared humanity. In the Confucian worldview, empathy creates harmony,
transforming relationships and strengthening
communities.

Consider the story of Emperor Wen of Han, who
was renowned for his compassion and leadership. When a harsh winter struck, he reduced
taxes and distributed food to the poor, empa-
thizing with the struggles of his people. His
actions earned their trust and loyalty, illustrat-
ing how empathy, when translated into action,
fosters both connection and respect.

The Neuroscience of Empathy

While Confucianism offers a philosophical
foundation for empathy, modern neuroscience
provides a scientific lens through which to understand its mechanisms. At the heart of empa-

thy lies the mirror neuron system, a network of neurons that activates when we observe someone else's actions or emotions. These neurons allow us to "feel" what others are experiencing, creating a biological basis for emotional connection.

For example, watching a friend receive good news might trigger a joyful response in your own brain, mirroring their happiness. Similarly, witnessing someone in pain can evoke a visceral reaction, motivating us to offer comfort. This neural mirroring highlights the deeply interconnected nature of human experience, reinforcing the idea that empathy is both innate and essential.

However, empathy is not automatic; it requires intention and effort. While our brains are wired for connection, biases, distractions, and emotional fatigue can hinder our ability to empathize. Strengthening empathy, therefore, involves cultivating habits that enhance our capacity to understand and relate to others.

Active Listening: The Gateway to Understand-

ing

One of the most effective ways to practice empathy is through active listening—a skill that requires us to fully engage with what another person is saying, without judgment or distraction. Active listening goes beyond hearing words; it involves observing tone, body language, and emotions to grasp the full context of the speaker's experience.

For instance, in a conversation with a colleague expressing frustration about a project, active listening might involve pausing to reflect on their concerns, asking clarifying questions, and responding with validation: "It sounds like you're feeling overwhelmed by the deadlines. How can I support you?" This approach not only demonstrates empathy but also fosters trust and collaboration.

Active listening is a cornerstone of emotional intelligence, as it encourages us to step outside our own perspective and enter someone else's. By practicing this skill, we create a safe space for others to share openly, deepening our connections and resolving misunderstandings.

Perspective-Taking: Expanding the Empathy Lens

Empathy also involves perspective-taking—the ability to see the world through someone else's eyes. This practice, emphasized in both philosophy and psychology, challenges us to move beyond our assumptions and consider the unique experiences and viewpoints of others.

Imagine a parent struggling to connect with their teenage child. Perspective-taking might involve reflecting on the pressures and uncertainties the teenager faces, from academic demands to social dynamics. By approaching the relationship with curiosity and understanding, the parent can foster a sense of empathy that bridges generational differences.

In a broader context, perspective-taking can help us navigate cultural or ideological divides. For example, during the Civil Rights Movement, activists like Martin Luther King Jr. emphasized the importance of understanding the experiences of marginalized communities. By encouraging society to empathize with the struggles of others, they inspired collective action and social change.

Perspective-taking requires humility and openness—a willingness to set aside our biases and embrace the complexity of human experience. When practiced consistently, it transforms relationships, creating deeper connections rooted in mutual respect.

The Role of Self-Awareness in Empathy

Empathy begins within. Self-awareness—the ability to recognize and understand our own emotions—provides the foundation for connecting with others. Without this inner clarity, our reactions may be clouded by unresolved feelings or biases, hindering our ability to empathize.

For example, a leader who is unaware of their own stress might respond impatiently to a team member seeking support. By cultivating self-awareness through practices like mindfulness or journaling, the leader can recognize their emotional state and approach the interaction with greater empathy and composure.

Self-awareness also enhances our ability to manage emotional boundaries. While empathy involves sharing in others' experiences, it does not mean absorbing their pain or neglecting our own needs. Striking this balance is key to sustaining emotional resilience and building healthy, supportive relationships.

Empathy in Action: Transforming Relationships

When empathy and emotional intelligence are woven into the fabric of our interactions, relationships flourish. Empathy transforms everyday moments into opportunities for connection, whether through a kind word, a thoughtful gesture, or simply being present. It is the glue that binds us together, fostering trust, understanding, and mutual support.

Consider a workplace setting where empathy is prioritized. A manager who listens to their employees' concerns, acknowledges their contributions, and offers encouragement creates an environment of collaboration and respect.

Similarly, in personal relationships, empathy strengthens bonds by allowing us to navigate challenges with compassion and grace.

Cultivating Empathy in Daily Life

Empathy is not a static trait but a skill that can be nurtured through intentional practice. Begin by pausing to reflect on your interactions: Are you truly listening, or are you focused on your response? Are you seeking to understand, or are you making assumptions? These questions guide us toward greater awareness and empathy.

Small acts, such as expressing gratitude, offering a genuine compliment, or checking in with someone who seems distressed, reinforce the habit of empathy. Over time, these actions create a ripple effect, inspiring others to approach their relationships with the same openness and care.

Conclusion

Empathy and emotional intelligence are not merely tools for navigating relationships; they are pathways to deeper connection and understanding. Through the insights of Confucian philosophy and modern neuroscience, we see that empathy is both an innate capacity and a cultivated practice. By listening actively, taking others' perspectives, and fostering self-awareness, we strengthen the bonds that unite us, transforming our relationships and enriching our lives. As we embrace empathy in action, we create a world where connection, compassion, and humanity thrive.

Building and Sustaining Trust

Trust is the invisible thread that holds relationships together, allowing them to flourish with authenticity, reliability, and depth. Without trust, even the strongest connections can falter, as suspicion and uncertainty erode the foundation of mutual respect. Trust is not a given; it is earned and nurtured over time through consistent actions, honest communication, and a commitment to ethical principles. As both a personal virtue and a relational cornerstone, trust enables meaningful connections to thrive.

The Philosophy of Trust: A Moral Obligation

Philosophers throughout history have recognized trust as essential to human relationships. Immanuel Kant, the 18th-century moral philosopher, argued that trust is grounded in the ethical principle of treating others as ends in themselves rather than as means to an end. For Kant, honesty and transparency are not just practical necessities but moral imperatives. When we act with integrity, we affirm the dignity of others and lay the groundwork for trust.

Similarly, in the works of Søren Kierkegaard, trust is viewed as an act of faith. For Kierkegaard, trust requires vulnerability—a willingness to rely on another while accepting the inherent risks of disappointment. This vulnerability is not a weakness but a testament to the courage and strength it takes to build genuine connections.

These philosophical insights remind us that trust is more than a transactional exchange; it is a moral and emotional investment in another person. By honoring our commitments and treating others with respect, we create an environment where trust can grow and endure.

The Elements of Trust: Reliability, Transparency, and Respect

Trust is built on three pillars: reliability, transparency, and respect. Each plays a vital role in fostering connections that stand the test of time.

Reliability is the foundation of trust. When we follow through on our promises and demonstrate consistency in our actions, we signal to others that they can depend on us. Consider a colleague who always meets deadlines and communicates openly about challenges. Their reliability fosters confidence and cooperation, strengthening the team's dynamic.

Transparency involves openness and honesty, even in difficult circumstances. This means not only sharing information but also being forthcoming about intentions and limitations. For example, a leader who admits to a mistake and outlines steps for improvement demonstrates humility and authenticity, earning the trust of their team.

Respect, the third pillar, is about valuing others' perspectives, boundaries, and experiences. Respect fosters an environment where people feel safe to express themselves without fear of judgment or dismissal. In a personal relationship, this might mean listening attentively to a partner's concerns and validating their emotions, even when disagreements arise.

Historical Lessons on Trust

History provides numerous examples of how trust has shaped relationships and influenced outcomes, both positive and negative. One striking example is the partnership between Franklin D. Roosevelt and Winston Churchill during World War II. Despite differences in background and political philosophy, their mutual trust and transparency forged a powerful alliance that helped guide the Allied forces to victory. Their correspondence, marked by candid discussions and shared resolve, exemplifies how trust can unite individuals in the pursuit of a common goal.

Conversely, the absence of trust can lead to devastating consequences. The Watergate scandal of the 1970s, which exposed corruption at the highest levels of American government, shattered public trust in leadership. This breach of trust eroded the social fabric, highlighting the fragility of relationships when transparency and accountability are lacking.

These examples underscore the dual nature of trust: its power to strengthen bonds and its vulnerability to betrayal. They remind us of the responsibility we bear in cultivating and preserving trust in our relationships.

Practical Strategies for Building Trust

While trust is intangible, it is built through tangible actions. One key strategy is practicing active accountability. This means taking ownership of our actions, acknowledging mistakes, and making amends when necessary. Accountability reinforces reliability and demonstrates a commitment to integrity.

For example, a manager who misses a deadline might proactively inform their team, explain the reasons for the delay, and outline a plan to prevent recurrence. By addressing the issue openly, they rebuild trust and model responsible behavior.

Another strategy is setting clear expectations. Ambiguity often breeds misunderstandings, which can undermine trust. In both personal and professional contexts, clear communication about goals, roles, and boundaries fosters mutual understanding and reduces the risk of conflict.

Trust also grows through small, consistent gestures that signal care and commitment. A parent attending their child's recital, a friend remembering a meaningful date, or a mentor providing timely feedback—these acts of attentiveness build a reservoir of goodwill that sustains relationships through challenges.

Repairing Trust After a Breach

Even in the most robust relationships, trust can

be tested or broken. When this happens, rebuilding trust requires effort, patience, and a willingness to address the underlying issues.

The first step is acknowledging the breach. Denying or minimizing the impact of broken trust only deepens the wound. Instead, a sincere apology, coupled with an acknowledgment of harm caused, demonstrates accountability and respect.

Next, actions must align with words. Rebuilding trust involves demonstrating consistent behavior that reinforces reliability and transparency. For example, in a partnership strained by dishonesty, open communication and a commitment to honesty over time can restore confidence.

Finally, trust repair requires forgiveness. This does not mean excusing harmful behavior but choosing to release resentment and create space for healing. Forgiveness is a collaborative process, requiring both parties to engage in dialogue and rebuild the relationship with intention.

The Role of Trust in Modern Relationships

In today's fast-paced, digital world, trust is more important than ever. With communication often mediated by technology, the potential for misunderstandings and misrepresentation increases. Building and sustaining trust requires intentional effort, from verifying information to demonstrating authenticity in online interactions.

Consider the dynamics of remote work, where trust plays a critical role in team cohesion. A leader who empowers their team with autonomy and supports open communication fosters an environment of trust, even across physical distances. Similarly, in personal relationships, trust is strengthened by consistent, meaningful interactions, whether through a heartfelt message or a shared experience.

Conclusion

Trust is the foundation of meaningful relationships, shaping how we connect, collaborate, and grow with others. Rooted in ethical principles and sustained through intentional actions, trust empowers us to navigate the complexities of human connection with confidence and grace. By embodying reliability, transparency, and respect, we create bonds that endure, transforming our relationships into sources of strength and fulfillment. As we build and sustain trust, we contribute not only to the well-being of those we care about but also to the integrity and harmony of the broader world.

Navigating Conflict with Grace

Conflict is an inevitable part of human relationships, arising from differences in values, priorities, and perspectives. While conflict can strain connections, it also presents an opportunity for growth and deeper understanding. Navigating these moments with grace requires compassion, humility, and effective communication—qualities that transform disagreements into constructive dialogues. Drawing from Buddhist teachings on compassion and modern conflict resolution techniques, we can approach conflict not as a threat but as a pathway to stronger relationships.

Buddhist Teachings: Compassion as the Foundation

Central to Buddhist philosophy is the principle of *karuna*, or compassion, which emphasizes understanding and alleviating the suffering of others. In the context of conflict, compassion encourages us to see beyond our own grievances and consider the emotions and experiences of the other party. By cultivating compassion, we soften the adversarial nature of disagreements and create space for empathy and connection.

The story of Siddhartha Gautama, the Buddha, offers a profound example of compassion in action. Faced with challenges and misunderstandings, the Buddha approached his detractors with patience and kindness, seeking to understand their concerns rather than react defensively. This mindset, rooted in non-attachment and equanimity, enabled him to resolve conflicts without animosity.

In modern relationships, practicing *karuna* means recognizing that conflict often stems from unmet needs or miscommunication. For instance, a heated argument between friends might be less about the surface issue and more about feelings of neglect or misunderstanding. By approaching the situation with compassion, we can uncover these deeper dynamics and address them constructively.

Humility: A Key to Resolving Conflict

Humility plays a crucial role in navigating conflict, as it allows us to acknowledge our own limitations and biases. Conflicts often escalate when individuals cling to the need to be "right," dismissing the validity of other perspectives. Humility, however, invites us to approach disagreements with an open mind, recognizing that our viewpoint is not the sole truth.

The philosopher Socrates modeled this principle through his method of inquiry, which involved asking questions to uncover underlying assumptions and foster mutual understanding. Socrates' humility in admitting what he did not know created an environment of curiosity rather than confrontation, encouraging constructive dialogue.

In practice, humility might mean stepping back during a disagreement to reflect on our own role in the conflict. Are we truly listening, or are we focused on defending our position? Are we open to the possibility that we might have misunderstood or contributed to the issue? This self-awareness fosters a sense of accountability, paving the way for resolution.

Open Communication: The Bridge to Understanding

Effective conflict resolution hinges on open communication, where both parties feel heard and valued. This involves not only expressing our own needs but also actively listening to the other person's perspective. Open communication transforms conflict from a zero-sum game into a collaborative effort to find common ground.

One technique for fostering open communication is the use of "I" statements, which focus on expressing feelings and needs without assigning blame. For example, instead of saying,

"You never listen to me," one might say, "I feel unheard when we don't take time to discuss my concerns." This shift in language reduces defensiveness and invites dialogue rather than escalation.

Another valuable approach is reflective listening, where we paraphrase the other person's words to ensure understanding. For instance, in a discussion with a colleague about workload, reflective listening might involve saying, "So, you're feeling overwhelmed because the deadlines are too tight. Is that right?" This technique demonstrates empathy and creates a foundation for collaborative problem-solving.

Modern Conflict Resolution Techniques

In addition to philosophical insights, modern conflict resolution techniques offer practical tools for navigating disagreements with grace. Mediation, for example, provides a structured process for facilitating dialogue between conflicting parties. Guided by a neutral mediator, individuals have the opportunity to express their concerns, explore underlying issues, and work toward mutually beneficial solutions.

The Harvard Negotiation Project's method of "principled negotiation" also offers valuable strategies. This approach emphasizes separating people from the problem, focusing on interests rather than positions, and exploring creative options for resolution. For example, in a dispute between neighbors over shared property, principled negotiation might shift the focus from "Who owns this space?" to "How can we both use this space effectively?"

These techniques align with the Buddhist emphasis on compassion and the philosophical focus on humility, reinforcing the idea that conflict resolution is not about winning but about fostering understanding and collaboration.

Learning from Historical Examples

History offers powerful examples of conflict resolution that demonstrate the transformative potential of compassion, humility, and communication. One such example is the leadership of Nelson Mandela, who navigated the deep divisions of apartheid-era South Africa with remarkable grace and resolve.

Rather than retaliate against those who had oppressed him, Mandela embraced reconciliation, fostering dialogue between opposing groups. His establishment of the Truth and Reconciliation Commission created a space for open communication, where individuals could share their experiences and seek accountability. Mandela's approach exemplifies the power of addressing conflict with compassion and humility, turning a nation's pain into a path toward healing.

In our own lives, these lessons remind us that even the most entrenched conflicts can be resolved when we prioritize connection over division. By approaching disagreements with an open heart and a willingness to listen, we create opportunities for transformation.

Preventing Conflict Through Proactive Practices

While conflict is inevitable, it can often be minimized through proactive relationship practices. Building trust, as explored in the previous section, creates a foundation of mutual respect

that reduces the likelihood of misunderstandings. Similarly, maintaining clear communication and addressing small issues before they
escalate helps prevent conflicts from becoming
entrenched.

Mindfulness is another valuable tool for conflict
prevention. By cultivating awareness of our
own emotions and reactions, we can respond to
potential triggers with greater calm and intentionality. For example, pausing to take a deep
breath before reacting to a critical comment
allows us to choose a measured response rather
than an impulsive one.

The Growth Potential of Conflict

When approached with grace, conflict becomes
an opportunity for growth. It challenges us to
confront our assumptions, expand our empathy,
and strengthen our relationships. While the
process of resolving conflict can be uncomfortable, it often leads to deeper understanding and
connection.

For instance, a disagreement between partners
about household responsibilities might initially

feel divisive. However, by engaging in open communication and exploring each other's perspectives, the partners can create a more equitable arrangement that enhances their relationship. Through this process, the conflict becomes a catalyst for positive change.

Conclusion

Navigating conflict with grace requires compassion, humility, and effective communication—qualities that transform disagreements into opportunities for connection and growth. By drawing from Buddhist teachings and modern conflict resolution techniques, we can approach conflicts with an open heart and a clear mind, fostering understanding and collaboration. In doing so, we not only strengthen our relationships but also cultivate the inner resilience needed to navigate the complexities of human connection. Conflict, when met with grace, becomes not a barrier but a bridge—a pathway to deeper understanding and mutual respect.

CHAPTER 6: THE DISCIPLINE OF HABITS – MASTERING DAILY ACTIONS

Philosophical Insights on Habits

Habits are the silent architects of our lives. They shape who we are and what we become, often without us fully realizing their influence. Aristotle, one of history's most profound thinkers, understood the power of habits long before modern science began to unravel their mechanisms. "We are what we repeatedly do," he wrote, linking daily actions to the cultivation of virtue and character. This insight, central to his philosophy of virtue ethics, remains as relevant today as it was in ancient Greece. By exploring the connection between Aristotle's teachings and modern research on habits, we gain a deeper understanding of how deliberate action can transform our lives.

Aristotle's Virtue Ethics: Habits as the Path to Excellence

For Aristotle, habits were not merely routines but the foundation of moral character. In his seminal work *Nicomachean Ethics*, he argued that virtues—qualities such as courage, generosity, and patience—are not innate traits but skills developed through consistent practice. Just as a musician becomes skilled through regular re-hearsal, an individual becomes virtuous by per-forming virtuous actions repeatedly. Habits, in this sense, are the building blocks of excellence.

Aristotle's perspective shifts the focus from iso-lated achievements to the ongoing process of self-improvement. He emphasized that great-ness is not a matter of chance or occasional effort but the result of consistent, intentional actions. "Excellence, then, is not an act but a habit," he concluded, highlighting the transformative power of repetition.

Consider the example of a leader striving to embody integrity. According to Aristotle, it is not enough to act honestly in a single instance; true integrity requires habitual honesty across countless decisions and interactions. Over time, these actions solidify into a reliable character, shaping the leader's identity and influence.

Modern Science and the Mechanics of Habits

While Aristotle provided a philosophical frame-work for understanding habits, modern research sheds light on their underlying mechanisms.

Neuroscientists and psychologists have identified habits as patterns of behavior driven by a cycle of cue, routine, and reward. This process, often referred to as the "habit loop," explains how behaviors become automatic over time.

For example, consider the habit of exercising in the morning. The alarm clock serves as the cue, the workout is the routine, and the sense of accomplishment or endorphin rush is the reward. Repeating this cycle consistently rewires the brain, making the behavior easier and more ingrained with each repetition.

James Clear, author of *Atomic Habits*, builds on this scientific foundation by emphasizing the cumulative power of small changes. Clear's "1% rule" suggests that improving by just 1% each day leads to remarkable growth over time. This principle aligns with Aristotle's assertion that excellence is achieved through incremental effort rather than dramatic leaps.

The Interplay of Habits and Character

The connection between habits and character is a recurring theme in both philosophy and modern psychology. Aristotle believed that habits shape not only our actions but also our desires and inclinations. By repeatedly choosing virtuous actions, we train ourselves to find joy and fulfillment in virtuous living. This process, known as habituation, aligns our inner values with our outward behavior.

Modern psychology echoes this idea through the concept of "behavioral congruence." When our actions align with our values, we experience a sense of integrity and well-being. Conversely, when our habits contradict our ideals, we may feel conflicted or dissatisfied. For instance, someone who values health but struggles with overeating may feel a disconnect between their goals and their daily actions. Cultivating habits that reflect their priorities—such as mindful eating or regular exercise—restores harmony between their aspirations and behavior.

This dynamic underscores the importance of intentionality in habit formation. While habits can develop passively, often shaped by external influences, conscious effort allows us to align our routines with our desired identity. By choosing habits that reflect our values, we take an active role in shaping our character and destiny.

Historical Examples of Habitual Excellence

Throughout history, individuals who achieved greatness often attributed their success to disciplined habits. Benjamin Franklin, one of America's founding fathers, famously outlined a daily schedule designed to cultivate virtues such as industry, humility, and temperance. Each day, Franklin reflected on his actions, identifying areas for improvement and reinforcing his commitment to personal growth. This practice, grounded in both philosophy and practicality, enabled him to achieve remarkable accomplishments in diverse fields.

Another powerful example is Olympic swimmer Michael Phelps, whose rigorous training regimen exemplifies the impact of habits on performance. Phelps' coach, Bob Bowman, emphasized consistency in every aspect of his preparation, from physical conditioning to mental visualization. Over years of practice, these habits became second nature, enabling Phelps to perform with precision under intense pressure.

Both Franklin and Phelps demonstrate that habits are not limited to moral development; they extend to every area of life, from professional success to physical health. Their stories remind us that mastery, in any domain, is built on a foundation of deliberate and consistent effort.

Practical Implications: Building Habits for a Purposeful Life

Aristotle's wisdom and modern science converge on a practical truth: the habits we cultivate today determine the life we lead tomorrow. This realization invites us to reflect on our current routines and consider how they align with our long-term goals and values. Are our habits moving us closer to the person we aspire to be, or are they holding us back?

One effective strategy for building positive habits is to start small and focus on consistency. Rather than overhauling one's lifestyle overnight, it is more sustainable to introduce incremental changes that build momentum. For example, someone seeking to improve their health might begin by walking for ten minutes each day, gradually increasing the duration and intensity over time.

Another approach is to identify "keystone habits"—routines that create a ripple effect, positively influencing other areas of life. For instance, regular exercise often leads to better sleep, improved focus, and healthier eating habits. By prioritizing these foundational practices, we amplify the benefits of habit formation.

Conclusion

Habits are the threads that weave the fabric of our lives, shaping our character, actions, and outcomes. Through Aristotle's virtue ethics and modern research, we gain a profound understanding of their power and potential. By cultivating intentional routines that reflect our values, we take an active role in our personal growth, transforming everyday actions into a path to excellence. In the words of Aristotle, "We are what we repeatedly do." Let us choose habits that align with our highest aspirations, allowing us to become the best versions of ourselves.

Building Positive Routines

Creating habits that align with our values and goals is one of the most powerful ways to shape a purposeful life. While the idea of building positive routines can feel daunting, it is a skill that anyone can develop with the right strategies and mindset. By approaching habit formation as a step-by-step process, grounded in both philosophy and practical tools, we can create a framework for lasting change. Techniques like habit stacking, incremental growth, and the intentional alignment of routines with personal values offer clear pathways to building a life of discipline and fulfillment.

The Role of Intention: Aligning Habits with Values

At the heart of habit formation lies intention. A positive routine is not merely a set of mechanical actions; it is a reflection of our deeper priorities and aspirations. The philosopher Epictetus, a proponent of Stoicism, emphasized the importance of aligning actions with values:

"First, say to yourself what you would be; and then do what you have to do." This guidance underscores the need to clarify our goals and let them inform our daily behaviors.

For example, someone who values lifelong learning might establish a habit of reading for 20 minutes each morning. This simple practice, rooted in intention, reinforces their commitment to growth and intellectual curiosity. By starting with a clear understanding of what matters most, we ensure that our routines are not just efficient but meaningful.

Habit Stacking: Building Momentum Through Association

One of the most effective strategies for creating positive routines is habit stacking, a concept popularized by James Clear in *Atomic Habits*. Habit stacking involves linking a new habit to an existing one, leveraging the momentum of the established routine to reinforce the new behavior. This technique works because it minimizes friction, making the new habit feel like a natural extension of an existing practice.

Consider the example of someone who wants to develop a gratitude practice. They might pair this new habit with brushing their teeth in the evening, taking a moment to reflect on three things they are grateful for before bed. Over time, this association strengthens, transforming the new habit into an automatic part of their routine.

Habit stacking also aligns with Aristotle's idea of habituation, where repeated actions create a ripple effect that shapes character. By building small, interconnected habits, we lay the groundwork for larger transformations, turning isolated routines into a cohesive system of growth.

The Power of Incremental Change: Start Small, Build Big

Incremental change is another cornerstone of effective habit formation. Rather than aiming for dramatic overhauls, which can feel overwhelming and unsustainable, starting with small, manageable steps allows us to build confidence and momentum. This approach is often referred to as the "two-minute rule," which encourages beginning a new habit with a version that takes no more than two minutes to complete.

For instance, someone aspiring to run a marathon might start by simply putting on their running shoes and stepping outside. This initial action lowers the barrier to entry, making it easier to follow through. Once the habit is established, it can naturally expand in scope and intensity.

Incremental change mirrors the principle of *kaizen*, a Japanese philosophy of continuous improvement. By focusing on small, consistent progress, we create a foundation for long-term success. Each step, no matter how modest, contributes to the larger goal, reinforcing a sense of achievement and forward momentum.

Creating Systems, Not Just Goals

While goals provide direction, systems ensure progress. A system is the structure that supports consistent action, making it easier to maintain positive routines over time. For example, someone striving to eat healthier might create a system by planning meals in advance, stocking their kitchen with nutritious options, and setting reminders for meal prep. This system reduces decision fatigue and creates an environment that supports their habit.

Philosopher William James recognized the importance of systems in habit formation, describing habits as "the flywheel of society." He argued that once a habit becomes automatic, it frees mental energy for higher pursuits. Systems play a critical role in this process by automating decision-making, allowing us to focus on execution rather than deliberation.

Overcoming Common Barriers to Positive Routines

Even with clear intentions and well-designed systems, obstacles can arise. Procrastination, lack of motivation, and external distractions often interfere with habit formation. Addressing these challenges requires both self-awareness and adaptability.

One effective strategy is to anticipate and plan for obstacles. For example, someone working to establish a morning meditation habit might identify potential barriers, such as staying up too late or hitting the snooze button. By preparing solutions—such as setting an earlier bedtime or placing the alarm clock across the room—they increase the likelihood of success.

Another approach is to focus on identity rather than outcomes. Instead of framing a habit as a task to complete, reframe it as an expression of who you are. For instance, rather than saying, "I need to exercise more," say, "I am someone who prioritizes health." This shift in mindset creates intrinsic motivation, making the habit feel like a natural extension of your identity.

The Role of Rewards in Reinforcing Habits

Positive reinforcement is a powerful tool for solidifying routines. By associating a habit with a rewarding experience, we strengthen the neural pathways that support the behavior. These rewards can be immediate, such as enjoying a favorite podcast during a workout, or long-term, such as tracking progress toward a milestone.

However, it is important to balance extrinsic

and intrinsic rewards. While external incentives can jumpstart a habit, intrinsic rewards—such as the satisfaction of living in alignment with one's values—are more sustainable over time. Reflecting on the deeper benefits of a habit, such as improved health or increased confidence, reinforces its significance and fosters lasting commitment.

Historical Examples of Positive Routines

Throughout history, many great thinkers and leaders have demonstrated the transformative power of positive routines. Benjamin Franklin's "virtue chart," where he tracked his adherence to specific habits each day, reflects the importance of intentional practice. Similarly, writer Maya Angelou maintained a disciplined writing routine, showing up daily to her rented workspace regardless of inspiration. These examples illustrate that consistency, more than perfection, is the key to success.

Conclusion

Building positive routines is a journey of intention, patience, and persistence. By aligning habits with our values, leveraging strategies like habit stacking and incremental change, and creating systems to support consistency, we lay the foundation for meaningful transformation. As Aristotle reminded us, "We are what we repeatedly do." Through deliberate action, we not only shape our daily lives but also cultivate the character and resilience needed to achieve our highest aspirations. Let each habit be a step toward the person you are destined to become.

Breaking Unproductive Patterns

Bad habits often cling to us like invisible chains, holding us back from achieving our potential and aligning our actions with our values. Whether it's procrastination, overeating, or negative self-talk, these patterns can feel deeply ingrained, leaving us frustrated by our inability to change. However, as challenging as breaking unproductive habits may seem, it is far from impossible. By understanding the psychological and philosophical roots of these behaviors, we can develop strategies to dismantle them and replace them with healthier, more empowering routines.

Understanding the Nature of Bad Habits

To break a bad habit, we must first understand how it forms and why it persists. Behavioral science identifies habits as the result of a loop involving cue, routine, and reward. For instance, the habit of scrolling through social media may begin with the cue of boredom, followed by the routine of opening an app, and ending with the reward of a brief dopamine hit. Over time, this loop becomes automatic, making the habit harder to break.

Philosophical teachings echo this insight by emphasizing the role of self-awareness in overcoming destructive behaviors. Socrates famously declared, "Know thyself," urging individuals to reflect on their actions and uncover the deeper motivations driving them. Often, bad habits are not just arbitrary behaviors but responses to unmet needs, unresolved emotions, or environmental triggers. By bringing these factors to light, we gain the clarity needed to address the root causes of our habits.

The Role of Willpower and Self-Mastery

Breaking a habit requires willpower, but it also demands a nuanced understanding of its limitations. Willpower, often described as the mental energy needed to resist temptation, is a finite resource. Studies in psychology suggest that relying solely on willpower is rarely effective for long-term change, as it can be depleted by stress, fatigue, and decision-making.

Philosophical teachings on self-mastery offer a broader perspective. The Stoics, for example, emphasized the importance of controlling one's impulses through reason and discipline. Epictetus advised, "No man is free who is not master of himself." This principle encourages us to cultivate self-awareness and intentionality, shifting the focus from resisting bad habits to replacing them with virtuous actions.

One practical application of this idea is reframing the concept of willpower. Instead of viewing it as the effort to suppress a behavior, we can see it as the commitment to align our actions with our values. For instance, someone who struggles with procrastination might focus not on resisting distractions but on fostering a sense of purpose and momentum in their work.

Practical Strategies for Breaking Bad Habits

Breaking unproductive patterns requires a combination of insight, planning, and action. One effective approach is to disrupt the habit loop by altering the cue or routine. For example, if the cue for late-night snacking is watching TV, replacing that activity with reading or meditation can break the association.

Another strategy is to make the bad habit less accessible or appealing. Behavioral economist Dan Ariely highlights the importance of "choice architecture," or designing environments that promote positive behaviors. For instance, keeping unhealthy snacks out of the house reduces the temptation to indulge, while placing exercise equipment in a visible location increases the likelihood of working out.

In addition to environmental changes, introducing friction can also help. If checking social media is a habit you want to break, adding steps—such as logging out of apps or turning off notifications—creates a barrier that disrupts automatic behavior.

Replacing Habits Instead of Eliminating Them

Philosophical and psychological insights converge on the idea that it's more effective to replace a bad habit than to eliminate it outright. The brain seeks to maintain the reward associated with a habit, so finding an alternative behavior that fulfills the same need is key.

For example, someone who smokes to relieve stress might replace smoking with deep breathing exercises or physical activity. These alternatives not only provide similar rewards but also reinforce healthier patterns over time. This principle is supported by the concept of neuroplasticity, which shows that the brain can form new neural pathways with consistent practice.

This approach aligns with Aristotle's virtue ethics, which emphasizes replacing vices with virtues. Instead of simply avoiding negative actions, we are encouraged to cultivate positive ones, shifting our focus from deprivation to growth.

The Power of Accountability and Support

Breaking bad habits is often more successful when approached with the support of others. Accountability creates a sense of external motivation, as we become more likely to follow through on commitments when someone else is aware of our goals. This principle can be seen in practices like sharing progress with a friend, joining a support group, or working with a mentor or coach.

Historical examples illustrate the power of collective accountability. In the early days of Alcoholics Anonymous (AA), members found strength in sharing their struggles and successes within a supportive community. This sense of connection helped individuals stay committed to their recovery, demonstrating the transformative impact of shared accountability.

For personal habits, creating an accountability system might involve enlisting a friend to check in regularly or using a habit-tracking app to monitor progress. These tools reinforce consistency and provide a sense of accomplishment, boosting motivation.

Overcoming Setbacks with Compassion

Breaking a bad habit is rarely a linear process. Setbacks are an inevitable part of the journey, but they do not signify failure. Instead, they offer valuable opportunities for learning and growth. When we approach setbacks with self-compassion, we create the emotional resilience needed to persist.

Buddhist teachings on compassion remind us to treat ourselves with kindness, even in the face of mistakes. The Dalai Lama once said, "If you lose your temper, do not blame yourself and feel bad about it. Instead, strive to improve with patience and diligence." This perspective encourages us to see setbacks as temporary and to remain focused on long-term progress.

For instance, if someone striving to reduce screen time finds themselves mindlessly scrolling one evening, they can reflect on what triggered the behavior and make adjustments for the future. This mindset transforms a setback into a stepping stone, reinforcing the commitment to change.

The Long-Term Benefits of Breaking Bad Habits

While the process of breaking unproductive patterns can be challenging, the rewards are profound. Removing habits that drain our energy, time, and focus creates space for growth, creativity, and fulfillment. It also strengthens our sense of agency, reminding us that we have the power to shape our lives through intentional action.

As we let go of old patterns, we open the door to new possibilities, aligning our daily behaviors with our highest aspirations. This transformation is not just about changing what we do but about becoming the person we wish to be.

Conclusion

Breaking bad habits is a journey of self-discovery, requiring a blend of awareness, strategy, and perseverance. By understanding the mechanisms that sustain unproductive patterns and applying practical techniques to disrupt them, we can reclaim control over our actions and choices. With the guidance of philosophical teachings and the support of modern behavioral science, we have the tools to overcome inertia and create a life that reflects our true values and potential. Let each step forward, however small, be a testament to your commitment to growth and self-mastery.

Sustaining Long-Term Discipline

Establishing a positive habit is only the beginning of a transformative journey. The real challenge lies in maintaining that habit over the long term, navigating the inevitable obstacles and fluctuations of life. Sustaining discipline requires more than sheer willpower; it calls for a blend of consistency, resilience, and adaptability. Through self-reflection, accountability, and an understanding of the broader purpose behind our actions, we can cultivate the endurance needed to make lasting change.

The Power of Consistency

Consistency is the cornerstone of habit sustainability. As Aristotle observed, "Excellence,
then, is not an act but a habit." The repetition of
positive actions over time not only strengthens
their presence in our lives but also deepens their
impact. Neuroscience supports this idea, revealing that repeated behaviors solidify neural
pathways, making habits more automatic and
less reliant on conscious effort.

Consider the example of a musician practicing
daily. Each session, no matter how short, contributes to the refinement of their skills. Even on
days when motivation wanes, the act of showing up reinforces the habit, building a foundation for future mastery. This principle applies
to all areas of life, from maintaining a fitness
routine to nurturing relationships. Small, consistent efforts accumulate, yielding results that
far outweigh isolated bursts of effort.

However, consistency is not about perfection.
Life's unpredictability means there will inevita-

bly be days when habits are disrupted. The key is to approach these moments with flexibility and a commitment to return to the habit as soon as possible. Missing one workout or skipping a meditation session does not undo progress; it is the decision to resume the routine that matters most.

Resilience in the Face of Setbacks

Resilience is the ability to adapt and persist despite challenges, and it plays a crucial role in sustaining habits over time. Philosophical teachings often highlight the importance of resilience in personal growth. Marcus Aurelius, the Stoic emperor, wrote, "The impediment to action advances action. What stands in the way becomes the way." This mindset transforms obstacles into opportunities, encouraging us to learn and grow from setbacks.

For instance, imagine someone striving to maintain a writing habit but facing writer's block. Rather than abandoning the practice, they might shift their focus to brainstorming ideas or revising previous work. By adapting their approach, they keep the momentum of the habit alive, even if the specific action changes.

Resilience also involves cultivating a growth mindset—the belief that abilities and habits can be developed through effort. Psychologist Carol Dweck's research shows that individuals with a growth mindset are more likely to persevere in the face of setbacks, viewing challenges as opportunities to improve rather than as evidence of failure. This perspective empowers us to maintain discipline, even when progress feels slow or difficult.

The Role of Self-Reflection

Sustaining long-term habits requires regular self-reflection to evaluate progress and make adjustments. Reflection allows us to identify what is working, address potential barriers, and reconnect with the purpose behind our habits. Without this practice, routines can become stagnant or disconnected from our evolving goals.

Journaling is one of the most effective tools for self-reflection. By recording thoughts, challenges, and achievements related to a habit, we gain valuable insights into our motivations and patterns. For example, someone committed to a fitness routine might journal about how exercise affects their mood and energy levels, reinforcing the benefits of the habit and providing motivation to continue.

Periodic reflection also helps us recognize and celebrate milestones. Acknowledging progress, no matter how small, reinforces the habit and builds confidence. For instance, a person learning a new language might reflect on their ability to hold a basic conversation, even if fluency remains a distant goal. These moments of recognition create a sense of achievement that fuels long-term commitment.

Accountability: The Social Dimension of Discipline

Accountability is a powerful motivator for sustaining habits. When we share our goals with others, we create a sense of external responsibility that complements our internal drive. This dynamic is evident in group settings such as fitness classes or professional development programs, where mutual accountability fosters consistency and support.

Historical examples illustrate the effectiveness
of accountability. The early meetings of Alcoholics Anonymous (AA) relied on peer support
to help members maintain sobriety. By sharing
their struggles and successes, participants built
a sense of community that reinforced their commitment to change.

In modern contexts, accountability can take
many forms. A friend or mentor might serve
as an accountability partner, checking in regularly to discuss progress. Digital tools, such as
habit-tracking apps or online communities, also
provide avenues for sharing goals and celebrating achievements. These mechanisms remind us
that we are not alone in our efforts, creating a
network of encouragement and motivation.

Revisiting Purpose and Vision

Long-term discipline thrives when it is rooted
in a clear sense of purpose. Habits that align
with our core values and aspirations are easier
to sustain because they carry intrinsic meaning. Reflecting on the "why" behind a habit

strengthens our commitment, especially during periods of doubt or difficulty.

For example, someone who has established a habit of saving money might revisit their vision of financial security or a specific goal, such as funding a family vacation. This reminder of purpose transforms the habit from a mundane task into a meaningful pursuit, reigniting motivation.

Philosophical teachings often emphasize the importance of purpose in sustaining action. Friedrich Nietzsche's famous assertion, "He who has a why to live can bear almost any how," speaks to the resilience that comes from aligning our actions with our deeper goals. By revisiting our purpose regularly, we ensure that our habits remain not only consistent but also meaningful.

Balancing Structure with Flexibility

While discipline relies on structure, it also requires flexibility to adapt to changing circumstances. Life's unpredictability means that rigid adherence to a habit may not always be possible. The key is to maintain the spirit of the habit, even if the specifics need to shift.

For instance, someone committed to a daily workout might substitute a shorter home session for a gym visit during a busy week. This adaptability preserves the habit's essence while accommodating external demands. Flexibility ensures that temporary disruptions do not derail long-term progress.

Conclusion

Sustaining long-term discipline is a journey of consistency, resilience, and purpose. By committing to regular practice, reflecting on progress, and seeking accountability, we create a framework that supports lasting change. Philosophical insights remind us that discipline is not about perfection but about persistence—the willingness to show up, adapt, and continue moving forward. With each step, we strengthen the habits that shape our lives, transforming daily actions into a legacy of growth and fulfillment. Let this commitment to discipline be a testament to your determination to lead a life aligned with your highest values and aspirations.

CHAPTER 7: ETHICAL LIVING – ALIGNING ACTIONS WITH VALUES

The Philosophy of Ethical Choices

Ethical living is the art of aligning our actions with our deepest values, ensuring that what we do reflects who we are and what we stand for. At its core, ethical living is not just about following rules or avoiding harm; it is about making deliberate choices that uphold integrity, fairness, and respect for others. Philosophical traditions from around the world provide timeless frameworks for navigating the complexities of moral decision-making, offering guidance on how to live a life that is both principled and purposeful.

Kant's Categorical Imperative: A Universal Standard

Immanuel Kant, an 18th-century German philosopher, sought to establish a universal foundation for ethics—one that transcended individual preferences and cultural norms. At the heart of Kant's philosophy lies the categorical imperative, a moral principle that asks us to act only in ways that could be universally applied. In essence, before making a decision, we are encouraged to ask ourselves: "What if everyone acted this way?"

Kant's categorical imperative is not just a thought experiment; it is a powerful tool for evaluating the ethical implications of our actions. For example, consider the act of lying. Kant argued that lying erodes trust, a fundamental building block of human relationships. If lying were universally accepted, trust would collapse, making meaningful connections impossible. Thus, the categorical imperative challenges us to uphold honesty, even when it is inconvenient or uncomfortable.

In modern life, Kant's framework offers clarity in situations where ethical boundaries may feel ambiguous. Imagine a professional facing pressure to exaggerate a product's capabilities to secure a sale. By applying the categorical imperative, they would recognize that such behavior, if universalized, would undermine trust in their industry, leading to long-term harm. This perspective encourages them to prioritize honesty, preserving their integrity and contributing to a culture of transparency.

Confucian Virtue Ethics: Cultivating Character

While Kant emphasized universal principles, Confucian philosophy takes a more relational approach to ethics, focusing on the cultivation of virtues that enhance harmony within families and communities. Central to Confucian thought is the concept of *ren*, often translated as "benevolence" or "humaneness." *Ren* embodies the idea of treating others with kindness, empathy, and respect, fostering relationships grounded in mutual care.

Confucius, the ancient Chinese philosopher, believed that ethical living begins with self-cultivation—the process of developing virtues such as honesty, humility, and compassion. He taught that individuals who embody these virtues naturally inspire others, creating a ripple effect of moral behavior. For Confucius, the family serves as the primary training ground for virtue, with the relationships between parents, children, and siblings offering daily opportunities to practice ethical living.

The Confucian emphasis on relationships provides valuable insights for navigating modern challenges. In the workplace, for instance, leaders who prioritize *ren* may focus not only on achieving results but also on fostering a supportive and inclusive environment. By treating employees with empathy and fairness, they build trust and loyalty, demonstrating that ethical leadership is as much about relationships as it is about outcomes.

The Intersection of Principles and Context

One of the enduring tensions in ethical decision-making is the balance between universal principles and contextual nuances. While frameworks like Kant's categorical imperative provide clear guidelines, real-life situations often involve competing values and complex dynamics. In these moments, ethical living requires both philosophical insight and practical wisdom.

Consider the example of a whistleblower who discovers unethical practices within their organization. From a Kantian perspective, exposing the truth aligns with the principle of honesty and accountability. However, the Confucian emphasis on relational harmony might highlight the potential harm to colleagues or the organization's reputation. Navigating this dilemma requires a thoughtful consideration of both principles and consequences, ensuring that the decision reflects a balance of integrity and compassion.

Philosophers like Aristotle offer guidance in such situations through the concept of *phronesis*, or practical wisdom. *Phronesis* involves applying ethical principles with discernment, taking into account the unique circumstances of each decision. It reminds us that ethical living is not about rigidly adhering to rules but about making choices that uphold our values while considering the broader impact.

Historical Examples of Ethical Leadership

Throughout history, individuals who exemplify ethical leadership have often relied on philosophical frameworks to guide their decisions. One such figure is Mahatma Gandhi, whose commitment to nonviolence (ahimsa) shaped his approach to social and political activism. Influenced by both Hindu and Jain teachings, Gandhi viewed nonviolence as a moral principle that extended beyond physical harm to include kindness in thought and speech. His adherence to this principle, even in the face of immense adversity, inspired millions and demonstrated the transformative power of ethical living.

Another example is Nelson Mandela, who prioritized reconciliation over retribution during South Africa's transition from apartheid. Mandela's decision to establish the Truth and Reconciliation Commission reflected a Confucian emphasis on relational harmony, as well as a Kantian commitment to justice. By creating a space for dialogue and accountability, Mandela fostered healing and unity, underscoring the importance of ethical choices in shaping a nation's future.

These leaders remind us that ethical living is not limited to grand gestures; it is woven into the fabric of our daily lives. Each decision, no matter how small, contributes to the character we build and the impact we leave on the world.

The Practical Application of Ethical Frameworks

Integrating philosophical frameworks into everyday decision-making begins with reflection. By taking time to clarify our values and principles, we create a moral compass that guides our actions. Journaling, meditation, or discussions with trusted mentors can help us identify what matters most and how we want to align our behavior with our beliefs.

Additionally, cultivating habits of mindfulness enhances our ability to act ethically in the moment. Mindfulness allows us to pause, consider the consequences of our actions, and choose responses that reflect our values. For example, in a heated argument, mindfulness might help us avoid reactive behavior, enabling us to communicate with respect and understanding.

Finally, ethical living thrives in community. Surrounding ourselves with individuals who share our commitment to integrity reinforces our values and provides support when challenges arise. Whether through professional networks, faith communities, or close friendships, these connections serve as anchors, reminding us of the shared responsibility to uphold ethical standards.

Conclusion

The philosophy of ethical choices offers a roadmap for aligning our actions with our values, empowering us to navigate life's complexities with integrity and purpose. From Kant's categorical imperative to Confucian virtue ethics, these frameworks illuminate the principles that guide moral decision-making, reminding us of our shared humanity and the impact of our choices. By integrating these insights into our daily lives, we not only elevate our own character but also contribute to a world that values fairness, empathy, and respect. Let every choice be a testament to the values we hold dear, shaping a life that reflects our highest aspirations.

Defining Personal Values

Defining personal values is a deeply introspective process that serves as the foundation for ethical living. These values act as a compass, guiding decisions and actions in a world often marked by uncertainty and complexity. While we all possess an innate sense of right and wrong, consciously identifying and clarifying our core values empowers us to live with intention, aligning our daily choices with the life we aspire to lead. This process is not merely a philosophical exercise; it is a practical and transformative journey toward authenticity and purpose.

The Importance of Values in Ethical Living

Values are the principles that define who we are and what we stand for. They shape how we respond to challenges, interact with others, and pursue our goals. When we act in alignment with our values, we experience a sense of integrity and coherence. Conversely, when our actions conflict with our values, we may feel dissonance or regret.

Philosophers and psychologists alike emphasize the importance of living in harmony with one's values. Viktor Frankl, a Holocaust survivor and author of *Man's Search for Meaning*, observed that individuals who derive meaning from their values are more resilient in the face of adversity. Frankl argued that even in the most challenging circumstances, the ability to align actions with a deeper purpose sustains hope and strength.

The role of values in ethical living can also be seen in Confucian philosophy, which emphasizes the cultivation of virtues such as honesty, respect, and compassion. For Confucius, these virtues are not abstract ideals but practical guides for harmonious living. By identifying our values and striving to embody them, we create a framework for navigating life's complexities with clarity and confidence.

The Process of Identifying Core Values

Defining personal values begins with introspection. Taking the time to reflect on what truly matters allows us to uncover the principles that resonate most deeply. This process can be facilitated through journaling, meditation, or guided exercises designed to illuminate our priorities and aspirations.

One effective exercise involves reflecting on

significant life experiences, both positive and negative, to identify recurring themes. For example, consider a moment when you felt a profound sense of fulfillment. What was happening? Who was involved? What values were being expressed? Similarly, think about a time when you felt deeply disappointed or conflicted. What values were being violated or neglected? These reflections often reveal patterns that point to core principles.

Another approach is to consider role models—individuals you admire for their character and actions. What qualities do they embody that inspire you? Whether it's integrity, courage, or kindness, these traits often mirror the values you aspire to cultivate in your own life.

Clarifying and Prioritizing Values

Once you have identified potential values, the next step is to clarify and prioritize them. Values are often interconnected, but understanding which ones hold the greatest significance helps to create a clear hierarchy for decision-making. For instance, if both family and career are important to you, determining which takes precedence in specific contexts can guide your choices when these priorities conflict.

One practical method for clarifying values is to create a personal mission statement—a concise declaration of your guiding principles and goals. For example, someone who values compassion and personal growth might write, "I strive to approach life with empathy, supporting others while continuously learning and improving myself." This statement serves as a touchstone, reminding you of your core values and their role in shaping your actions.

Philosopher John Stuart Mill's principle of utility can also inform this process. Mill suggested that ethical decisions should aim to maximize happiness and well-being, both for oneself and others. Applying this principle to personal values encourages a broader perspective, prompting us to consider not only what aligns with our individual aspirations but also what contributes to the greater good.

The Role of Alignment in Living a Purposeful

Life

Defining values is only the beginning; the true challenge lies in aligning our actions with those values. This alignment requires both intention and discipline, as it often involves making choices that prioritize long-term fulfillment over short-term convenience.

For example, someone who values health and well-being might choose to forgo unhealthy foods or establish a regular exercise routine. While these decisions may require effort and sacrifice in the moment, they reflect a commitment to living in harmony with their values, leading to greater satisfaction over time.

Similarly, aligning actions with values can deepen relationships and foster trust. Consider a leader who values transparency and fairness. By consistently communicating openly and treating others equitably, they build a reputation for integrity, inspiring loyalty and respect among their team. This alignment between values and actions not only enhances personal fulfillment but also contributes to a positive impact on others.

Overcoming Challenges in Defining and Living by Values

Defining and living by values is not always straightforward. External pressures, societal expectations, and competing priorities can create conflicts that make it difficult to stay true to one's principles. In these moments, self-awareness and resilience are essential.

Philosophical teachings offer guidance for navigating these challenges. The Stoics, for instance, emphasized the importance of focusing on what is within our control. According to Marcus Aurelius, "You have power over your mind—not outside events. Realize this, and you will find strength." By concentrating on our internal choices and responses, we can remain grounded in our values, even when external circumstances are beyond our influence.

Practicing mindfulness can also help. By cultivating present-moment awareness, we become more attuned to our intentions and actions, allowing us to identify and address misalignments before they escalate. For example, if a busy schedule begins to encroach on time spent with loved ones, mindfulness can prompt a reassessment of priorities, ensuring that relationships remain a central focus.

The Transformative Impact of Defining Values

Defining and living by personal values is a transformative process that extends far beyond individual decisions. When we act in alignment with our principles, we create a ripple effect that inspires others and contributes to a more ethical and compassionate world. Just as a stone dropped into a pond creates concentric waves, our choices influence the people and environments around us, demonstrating the power of values in action.

Historical figures like Eleanor Roosevelt exemplify this impact. Known for her advocacy of human rights and social justice, Roosevelt's actions consistently reflected her deeply held values of equality and empathy. Her life serves as a reminder that defining and living by values not only enhances personal fulfillment but also creates a legacy of positive change.

Conclusion

Defining personal values is a journey of self-discovery that lays the foundation for ethical living and purposeful action. Through introspection, reflection, and intentional alignment, we uncover the principles that guide our lives, empowering us to make decisions with clarity and integrity. While the path may involve challenges and complexities, the rewards—greater authenticity, fulfillment, and impact—are immeasurable. Let this process be a testament to the power of values in shaping a life of meaning and significance.

Navigating Ethical Dilemmas

Ethical dilemmas often arise when two or more values come into conflict, challenging us to make decisions that honor our principles without compromising our integrity. These moments are rarely straightforward; they require careful thought, emotional resilience, and a willingness to embrace complexity. Whether in personal relationships, professional settings, or societal roles, navigating ethical dilemmas is a skill that can be developed through philosophical insight and practical strategies.

The Nature of Ethical Dilemmas

Ethical dilemmas test the boundaries of our values, revealing the nuanced nature of moral decision-making. Unlike clear-cut choices, dilemmas involve competing priorities that each hold weight. For example, consider a parent torn between spending time with their family and working overtime to provide financial stability. Both choices reflect deeply held values—family connection and responsibility—but fulfilling one may come at the expense of the other.

Philosophers have long explored the tension inherent in ethical dilemmas. Jean-Paul Sartre, a leading figure in existentialism, highlighted the anguish of choice in his writings. He argued that individuals are free to make decisions but must also bear the responsibility for their consequences. This perspective encourages us to approach dilemmas with a sense of ownership, recognizing that our choices shape not only our lives but also the lives of those around us.

Philosophical Frameworks for Resolving Dilemmas

To navigate ethical dilemmas effectively, it is helpful to draw on philosophical frameworks that provide clarity and structure. Utilitarianism, for instance, emphasizes the principle of maximizing well-being. Proposed by philosophers Jeremy Bentham and John Stuart Mill, this approach evaluates the consequences of actions, seeking to choose the option that produces the greatest good for the greatest number.

While utilitarianism offers a practical lens for decision-making, it can sometimes conflict with other ethical principles, such as individual rights or justice. Kant's deontological ethics, in contrast, focuses on the inherent morality of actions rather than their outcomes. According to Kant, certain actions, such as telling the truth, are morally obligatory regardless of the consequences. Applying this framework to a dilemma requires examining whether the chosen action aligns with universal principles of fairness and respect.

Another valuable perspective comes from virtue ethics, which emphasizes the character of the decision-maker rather than specific rules or outcomes. Aristotle argued that ethical dilemmas should be resolved by cultivating virtues such as courage, compassion, and wisdom. From this viewpoint, the process of navigating a dilemma becomes an opportunity for personal growth, as each choice reflects and reinforces our moral character.

Real-World Examples of Ethical Dilemmas

History is filled with examples of individuals facing profound ethical dilemmas, their decisions offering valuable lessons in moral courage and discernment. During World War II, Oskar Schindler, a German industrialist, faced the harrowing choice of profiting from the war effort or risking his safety to save the lives of Jewish workers. Guided by his growing sense of compassion and justice, Schindler chose the latter, using his resources to shield over 1,200 people from persecution. His story demonstrates the transformative power of aligning actions with deeply held values, even in the face of immense personal risk.

In contemporary contexts, ethical dilemmas often arise in professional settings. Consider a whistleblower who uncovers unethical practices within their organization. Reporting the misconduct aligns with principles of honesty and accountability, but it may also jeopardize their career or relationships with colleagues. Navigating this dilemma requires balancing personal integrity with the potential consequences, a process that can be guided by both philosophical reflection and practical support systems.

Practical Strategies for Navigating Ethical Dilemmas

While philosophical frameworks provide a foundation for understanding dilemmas, practical strategies help translate these insights into action. One effective approach is to engage in reflective questioning, exploring the implications of each potential choice. For example:

- What values are at stake in this decision?
- How will my choice affect others, both imme-

diately and in the long term?
- Does this action align with my principles, or am I compromising them for convenience or pressure?

These questions encourage deeper awareness, allowing us to weigh options thoughtfully rather than reacting impulsively.

Another strategy is to seek diverse perspectives. Ethical dilemmas often feel isolating, but discussing them with trusted mentors, colleagues, or friends can provide clarity. Different viewpoints illuminate blind spots and offer new angles for consideration, enriching the decision-making process. However, it is essential to choose confidants who respect your values and share your commitment to integrity.

The Role of Emotional Intelligence

Navigating ethical dilemmas requires not only intellectual rigor but also emotional intelligence—the ability to understand and manage emotions in oneself and others. Emotional intelligence helps us stay grounded in the face of difficult decisions, fostering empathy and self-awareness. For example, a manager re-solving a conflict between team members must balance fairness with compassion, addressing the situation in a way that respects everyone involved.

Mindfulness practices can enhance emotion-al intelligence by cultivating present-moment awareness and reducing reactivity. When faced with a dilemma, pausing to breathe deeply and reflect creates space for thoughtful responses rather than impulsive reactions. This mindful-ness also allows us to recognize and address underlying emotions, such as fear or guilt, that may cloud our judgment.

Accepting Imperfection in Ethical Decisions

Ethical dilemmas rarely have perfect solutions. Accepting this reality can alleviate the pressure to find a "right" answer and instead focus on making the best possible choice under the cir-cumstances. Philosopher Søren Kierkegaard described this acceptance as a "leap of faith," acknowledging that uncertainty is an inherent part of human experience. By embracing the ambiguity of dilemmas, we free ourselves to act with courage and authenticity, trusting that our intentions and values will guide us.

This perspective is particularly relevant in fast-paced or high-stakes environments, where time constraints may limit deliberation. In such cases, relying on well-cultivated habits of ethical reflection and decision-making can provide a steady anchor, enabling us to act decisively without compromising our principles.

The Growth Potential of Ethical Dilemmas

While ethical dilemmas are often challenging, they also offer opportunities for growth and transformation. Each decision, no matter how difficult, strengthens our moral character and deepens our understanding of ourselves and others. By reflecting on the outcomes of past dilemmas, we refine our values and build the resilience needed to face future challenges with confidence.

For example, someone who navigates a professional conflict with integrity may emerge not only with a stronger sense of self but also with enhanced leadership skills and deeper trust from their colleagues. These experiences shape our character, reminding us that ethical living is a continuous journey rather than a fixed destination.

Conclusion

Navigating ethical dilemmas is a complex but rewarding process that calls on us to integrate philosophical wisdom, emotional intelligence, and practical strategies. By drawing on frameworks such as utilitarianism, deontology, and virtue ethics, we gain clarity in the face of competing values. Through self-reflection, dialogue, and a commitment to integrity, we make choices that align with our principles while honoring the complexities of life. Each dilemma we encounter becomes an opportunity to grow, deepen our understanding, and strengthen the foundation of our ethical living. Let these moments of challenge serve as milestones on the path to a life of purpose and authenticity.

Leading by Example

Ethical living is not only a personal endeavor; it has the power to inspire and influence others, creating ripples of integrity that extend far beyond individual actions. When we lead by example, we embody the principles we wish to see in the world, demonstrating that values-driven behavior is both possible and impactful. This type of leadership is grounded in authenticity, moral courage, and a commitment to the greater good. It invites others to reflect on their own choices, fostering a culture of ethical awareness and accountability.

The Transformative Power of Leading by Example

Leading by example begins with living in alignment with one's values. This authenticity resonates deeply with others, as actions often speak louder than words. Philosophers like Laozi, the founder of Taoism, emphasized the subtle yet profound influence of ethical leadership. He wrote, "A leader is best when people barely know they exist... when their work is done, their aim fulfilled, they will say: We did it ourselves." This perspective highlights the power of quiet, consistent integrity in shaping the attitudes and behaviors of others.

In everyday life, leading by example can take many forms. A teacher who prioritizes fairness and compassion fosters an environment of respect among students. A manager who emphasizes transparency and accountability sets a standard for ethical conduct within their team. These actions, though seemingly small, create a ripple effect, inspiring others to embody similar principles in their own interactions.

Historical Figures as Ethical Leaders

History offers countless examples of individuals whose ethical leadership inspired transformative change. Mahatma Gandhi's philosophy of nonviolence, or *ahimsa*, stands as a powerful testament to the impact of leading by example. Gandhi's commitment to nonviolence was not merely a political strategy but a way of life. By refusing to meet oppression with aggression, he demonstrated the moral strength of peaceful resistance, inspiring millions to join the struggle for India's independence. His actions proved that ethical living is not passive but an active force for change, capable of dismantling injustice and fostering unity.

Another notable figure is Nelson Mandela, who prioritized reconciliation over retribution during South Africa's transition from apartheid. After spending 27 years in prison, Mandela emerged with a message of forgiveness and inclusion, choosing to lead by example rather than succumb to bitterness or revenge. His decision to establish the Truth and Reconciliation Commission reflected a commitment to healing and justice, setting the tone for a nation seeking to rebuild itself. Mandela's ethical leadership not only shaped South Africa's future but also inspired global admiration for his moral courage and vision.

The Ripple Effect of Ethical Actions

The influence of leading by example extends far beyond immediate circles, creating a ripple effect that touches lives in unexpected ways. Ethical actions inspire trust, encourage collaboration, and foster a sense of shared responsibility. For example, a business leader who prioritizes environmental sustainability may inspire employees, customers, and competitors to adopt similar practices, amplifying the impact of their choices.

This ripple effect is particularly evident in social movements, where ethical leaders serve as catalysts for collective action. Dr. Martin Luther King Jr., a central figure in the American civil rights movement, exemplified this dynamic. Through his unwavering commitment to justice, nonviolence, and equality, King inspired a generation to challenge systemic racism and advocate for human rights. His leadership was not about commanding followers but about empowering them to embrace their own moral agency, transforming individual values into collective change.

The Challenges of Leading by Example

While leading by example is profoundly impactful, it is not without challenges. Ethical leaders often face scrutiny, resistance, and personal sacrifice. Remaining steadfast in the face of adversity requires moral courage and resilience. Socrates, one of the most influential philosophers in Western history, exemplified this courage. Charged with corrupting the youth and impiety, Socrates chose to uphold his principles rather than compromise for personal safety. His decision to accept the death penalty rather than renounce his beliefs demonstrated an unwavering commitment to truth and integrity, leaving a legacy that continues to inspire.

In modern contexts, ethical leadership may involve navigating difficult choices that challenge personal or professional interests. For instance, a whistleblower who exposes corporate misconduct embodies ethical courage but may face significant professional and social repercussions. Despite these challenges, their actions highlight the transformative power of prioritizing the greater good over individual gain.

Practical Applications of Leading by Example

Leading by example is not limited to extraordinary circumstances or historical figures; it is a practice that can be cultivated in everyday life. The first step is to consistently align actions with values, ensuring that behavior reflects principles such as honesty, empathy, and fairness. This alignment builds trust and credibility, reinforcing the authenticity of one's leadership.

Creating opportunities for dialogue and collaboration further enhances the impact of ethical leadership. By engaging others in conversations about values and ethics, leaders encourage reflection and shared accountability. For example, a community organizer might hold workshops on environmental stewardship, inviting participants to explore how their choices impact the planet. These initiatives foster a sense of collective responsibility, empowering individuals to contribute to positive change.

Mentorship is another powerful avenue for leading by example. By guiding and supporting others, ethical leaders pass on their principles and practices, nurturing a new generation of conscientious individuals. This mentorship can take many forms, from formal coaching relationships to informal acts of encouragement and advice.

The Legacy of Ethical Leadership

The true measure of ethical leadership lies in its enduring legacy. Leaders who act with integrity and courage leave behind more than accomplishments; they inspire others to carry forward their values, creating a ripple effect that spans generations. This legacy is evident in figures like Eleanor Roosevelt, who championed human rights and social justice throughout her life. As the driving force behind the Universal Declaration of Human Rights, Roosevelt's leadership continues to shape global conversations about dignity and equality.

Ethical leadership also shapes the culture of organizations and communities, setting standards that endure long after the leader's tenure. A company founded on principles of fairness and transparency, for example, may maintain these values through successive generations of leadership, fostering trust and loyalty among employees and stakeholders.

Conclusion

Leading by example is one of the most powerful ways to inspire ethical living and create meaningful change. By aligning actions with values, ethical leaders demonstrate the transformative potential of integrity, encouraging others to reflect on their own choices and contributions. From historical figures like Gandhi and Mandela to everyday acts of mentorship and collaboration, the ripple effects of ethical leadership remind us that our actions matter—not only for ourselves but for the world around us. Let this commitment to leading by example serve as a beacon, guiding others toward a life of purpose, authenticity, and shared humanity.

CHAPTER 8: THE LEGACY YOU LEAVE – LIVING WITH PURPOSE

Embracing Mortality

Mortality is one of life's most profound and inescapable truths. While the awareness of death may seem daunting, it has long served as a source of inspiration for philosophers, spiritual leaders, and thinkers who view it not as a cause for despair but as a catalyst for living with greater purpose. To truly embrace mortality is to acknowledge the impermanence of life, allowing this understanding to inform our actions and priorities. By confronting the finite nature of our existence, we can gain clarity, focus, and the resolve to live meaningfully.

The Stoic Perspective: Memento Mori

For the Stoics, mortality was a central theme in their philosophy. The phrase *memento mori,* meaning "remember you must die," encapsulates their view that reflecting on death is essential to living a virtuous life. Rather than avoiding thoughts of mortality, the Stoics encouraged daily contemplation of life's fragility as a means of fostering gratitude and resilience.

Seneca, a Roman statesman and philosopher,

frequently wrote about the importance of accepting death as a natural part of life. In his essay *On the Shortness of Life*, he argued that life is long enough if it is lived wisely. According to Seneca, much of life's perceived brevity arises from squandering time on trivial pursuits. By reflecting on death, we are reminded to focus on what truly matters—our relationships, our contributions, and our inner growth.

Marcus Aurelius, another prominent Stoic, expressed similar sentiments in his *Meditations*. He advised readers to live each day as if it were their last, not with recklessness but with a sense of intentionality and presence. For Marcus, death was not an end to be feared but a transition to be accepted, one that places the value of each moment into sharp relief. This mindset encourages us to live fully, unencumbered by regret or procrastination.

Buddhist Teachings on Impermanence

In Buddhism, the concept of impermanence (*anicca*) is a cornerstone of spiritual practice. Buddhists view the transient nature of life as a reality to be embraced rather than resisted.

By meditating on impermanence, practitioners cultivate a sense of detachment from material possessions and external circumstances, focusing instead on inner peace and compassion.

The Tibetan Buddhist practice of *maranasati*, or mindfulness of death, exemplifies this approach. Monks often meditate on images of decay or recite verses reminding them of life's impermanence. While these practices may seem morbid, their purpose is to awaken a deeper appreciation for life. By recognizing that all things are temporary, practitioners are inspired to live with greater mindfulness and generosity, making the most of the time they have.

The story of the Buddha's enlightenment also underscores the role of mortality in inspiring transformation. Before achieving enlightenment, Siddhartha Gautama encountered the "Four Sights," which included an old man, a sick person, and a corpse. These encounters revealed the inevitability of aging, illness, and death, prompting Siddhartha to seek a path to liberation. His journey reminds us that awareness of mortality can be a powerful motivator for self-discovery and purposeful action.

How Mortality Shapes Purpose

Embracing mortality compels us to ask fundamental questions about how we wish to spend
our time and energy. What legacy do we want
to leave? How do we want to be remembered by
those whose lives we touch? These reflections
guide us toward living with greater authenticity
and intention.

Consider the story of Steve Jobs, the visionary
co-founder of Apple. In his widely celebrated
commencement speech at Stanford University,
Jobs shared how his awareness of death influenced his decisions and priorities. "Remembering that I'll be dead soon," he said, "is the
most important tool I've ever encountered to
help me make the big choices in life." For Jobs,
the recognition of mortality stripped away distractions and fears, allowing him to focus on
what he truly valued: creativity, innovation, and
meaningful work.

This perspective resonates not only with
high-profile figures but also with everyday indi-

viduals who use the awareness of death to find clarity. A person who faces a serious illness, for instance, often gains a newfound appreciation for life's simple joys and a sharper sense of what truly matters. These moments of reckoning reveal that purpose is not found in accumulating wealth or status but in the connections we build, the kindness we show, and the impact we have on others.

Practical Applications: Living with Awareness of Mortality

While mortality may seem like an abstract concept, there are practical ways to integrate this awareness into daily life, fostering a sense of purpose and urgency. One powerful exercise is writing your own eulogy. This practice encourages you to envision the legacy you want to leave behind and the values you hope to embody. By imagining how you would like to be remembered, you gain insight into the choices and actions that align with your deeper aspirations.

Another approach is to adopt the Stoic practice of reflecting on death each morning or evening.

This can be as simple as reminding yourself that today is a gift, not guaranteed, and asking how you can make the most of it. Such reflections shift your focus from trivial concerns to meaningful pursuits, whether that means reaching out to a loved one, contributing to your community, or pursuing a long-held dream.

Mindfulness meditation also offers a way to connect with the present moment, embracing life's impermanence without fear or denial. By cultivating awareness of the here and now, you develop the capacity to savor each experience, no matter how ordinary. This practice reinforces the understanding that life's beauty lies in its fleeting nature.

The Freedom of Accepting Mortality

Paradoxically, accepting mortality can be liberating. When we let go of the illusion of permanence, we free ourselves from the anxiety of clinging to what cannot be preserved. This freedom allows us to live with greater spontaneity, courage, and generosity, knowing that our time is finite but full of potential.

Philosopher Martin Heidegger described this state as "being-toward-death," a way of living authentically by acknowledging life's temporality. According to Heidegger, confronting death strips away superficial distractions, revealing the essence of what it means to be truly alive. This perspective encourages us to embrace life not despite its impermanence but because of it.

Conclusion

Embracing mortality is not about dwelling on death but about illuminating life. By confronting the reality of impermanence, we gain a clearer sense of purpose, focusing on what truly matters and letting go of what does not. Whether through Stoic meditations, Buddhist teachings, or personal reflection, the awareness of mortality invites us to live fully, with intention and gratitude. Let this acceptance serve as a guide, reminding us that while life may be finite, its potential for meaning and impact is boundless.

Defining Your Legacy

Every life leaves a mark, whether intentional or unintentional. The way we choose to interact with others, the values we uphold, and the actions we take all contribute to the legacy we leave behind. Defining your legacy is not about grand achievements or public accolades—it is about understanding the impact you want to have on those around you and the world at large. By consciously shaping your legacy, you create a life that aligns with your values and aspirations, leaving behind a testament to the principles you hold dear.

The Meaning of Legacy

Legacy is more than material wealth or tangible accomplishments; it is the lasting impression we leave on others through our character, actions, and relationships. It encompasses the memories we create, the values we instill, and the contributions we make to our communities and society. As Maya Angelou beautifully expressed, "Your legacy is every life you've ever touched."

From a philosophical perspective, legacy is a

bridge between the finite nature of our lives and the enduring impact of our choices. The Stoics believed that while we cannot control our mortality, we can control the influence we leave behind through virtuous living. Marcus Aurelius, in his *Meditations*, encouraged readers to act in a way that reflects their highest principles, knowing that their deeds will echo beyond their lifetime.

Similarly, existentialist philosophers like Jean-Paul Sartre emphasized the importance of creating meaning through our actions. Sartre argued that our choices define who we are and shape the world we inhabit. This perspective underscores the responsibility we bear in crafting a legacy that reflects our authentic selves and contributes to the greater good.

Reflecting on the Legacy You Want to Leave

Defining your legacy begins with introspection. Reflecting on questions about your values, priorities, and aspirations helps clarify the impact you wish to have. What principles guide your decisions? What do you want to be remembered for? How do you hope to influence those whose lives you touch? These questions provide a foundation for envisioning a meaningful legacy.

One effective practice is to write your own obituary or eulogy. This exercise encourages you to imagine how you would like others to describe your life and character. Did you live with kindness and integrity? Did you inspire others to pursue their dreams? By articulating these aspirations, you gain a clearer sense of the actions and attitudes needed to align your present life with your desired legacy.

Another approach is to identify role models whose legacies resonate with you. Reflecting on the lives of individuals who embody qualities you admire can provide valuable insights into the kind of impact you wish to have. Whether it is the compassion of Mother Teresa, the courage of Nelson Mandela, or the creativity of Leonardo da Vinci, these examples offer inspiration for shaping your own path.

Aligning Legacy with Values

Once you have envisioned your legacy, the next step is to ensure that it aligns with your core values. Living authentically means letting your values guide your decisions and interactions. For example, if you value empathy and generosity, your legacy might center on acts of kindness, supporting others in times of need, or fostering inclusivity in your community.

Aristotle's concept of eudaimonia, often translated as "flourishing," emphasizes the fulfillment that comes from living in accordance with one's virtues. According to Aristotle, a meaningful life is not measured by external success but by the cultivation of qualities such as wisdom, courage, and justice. Applying this principle to legacy means focusing on the intangible ways you enrich the lives of others and contribute to the well-being of society.

Consider the legacy of Fred Rogers, the beloved creator of *Mister Rogers' Neighborhood*. Rogers' life was a testament to his values of kindness, respect, and emotional connection. Through his gentle demeanor and thoughtful words, he inspired generations of children and adults to approach life with compassion and understanding. His legacy endures not because of wealth or accolades but because of the values he consistently lived and shared.

The Role of Purpose in Shaping Legacy

Purpose is the driving force behind a meaningful legacy. When we live with a sense of purpose, our actions take on greater significance, contributing to a narrative that extends beyond ourselves. Viktor Frankl, a Holocaust survivor and author of *Man's Search for Meaning*, argued that purpose arises from our commitments to something greater than ourselves—whether it is a cause, a community, or a creative pursuit.

Frankl's philosophy is a reminder that legacy is not about perfection but about intention. We do not need to have all the answers or achieve extraordinary feats to make a difference. Small, consistent actions driven by purpose can have a profound impact over time. Whether it is mentoring a younger colleague, volunteering in your community, or simply being present for loved ones, these moments of purpose add up to a legacy of meaning and connection.

Practical Steps for Defining Your Legacy

Defining your legacy is an ongoing process that evolves with your experiences and growth. To begin this journey, consider incorporating reflective practices into your routine. Journaling, for instance, allows you to explore your thoughts and feelings about the kind of impact you want to have. Questions like "What am I proud of today?" and "How did I contribute to others?" encourage introspection and alignment with your values.

Another practical step is to create a vision board or timeline that outlines the legacy you hope to build. Visualizing your aspirations helps translate abstract ideas into concrete goals, providing motivation and direction. For example, if your legacy involves supporting education, you might set milestones for mentoring students, contributing to scholarships, or advocating for educational reform.

Engaging in open conversations with family, friends, and colleagues can also deepen your understanding of your legacy. Sharing your intentions and listening to others' perspectives fosters a sense of accountability and collaboration, reinforcing your commitment to living in alignment with your values.

The Ripple Effect of a Thoughtful Legacy

When we consciously define and pursue our legacy, its impact extends far beyond ourselves. Ethical actions and meaningful contributions inspire others to reflect on their own values and aspirations, creating a ripple effect of positive change. This phenomenon is evident in the lives of figures like Jane Goodall, whose work in conservation and animal rights has inspired countless individuals to care for the planet and its inhabitants.

Your legacy does not need to be grand or far-reaching to be meaningful. A parent who instills a love of learning in their child, a friend who offers unwavering support during difficult times, or a neighbor who fosters a sense of community—all of these acts contribute to a legacy that enriches the lives of others.

Conclusion

Defining your legacy is an invitation to live with purpose and intention. By reflecting on your values, envisioning the impact you want to have, and aligning your actions with your aspirations, you create a life that resonates with meaning and authenticity. Whether through small gestures or significant endeavors, your legacy is a testament to the principles you hold dear and the difference you make in the world. Let this process inspire you to live fully, embracing each moment as an opportunity to shape the story you leave behind.

Living with Intention

Living with intention is the art of aligning our daily actions with our long-term purpose. It is about moving beyond routine and inertia to live deliberately, with a clear sense of what matters most. This approach to life is both empowering and transformative, enabling us to create meaning and fulfillment in our experiences. By adopting practices rooted in mindfulness and proactive decision-making, we can ensure that each moment contributes to the legacy we wish to leave.

The Philosophy of Intentional Living

Intentional living has deep philosophical roots. Aristotle's concept of *telos*—the idea that everything has an inherent purpose—reminds us that living well requires understanding and striving toward our ultimate goals. For Aristotle, happiness and fulfillment arise not from fleeting pleasures but from consistently making choices that align with our virtues and aspirations.

Similarly, existentialist thinkers like Jean-Paul Sartre and Simone de Beauvoir emphasized the importance of taking responsibility for our choices. Sartre argued that life's meaning is not predetermined; it is something we must create through our actions. To live with intention, then, is to take ownership of our decisions, recognizing that each one shapes the story of our lives.

Modern thinkers echo these sentiments. Stephen Covey, in his influential book *The 7 Habits of Highly Effective People*, urges readers to "begin with the end in mind." This principle encourages us to visualize our desired outcomes and use them as a guide for making intentional choices. By focusing on what truly matters, we can ensure that our actions contribute to a life of significance.

Mindfulness as the Foundation of Intention

At the heart of living with intention lies mindfulness—the practice of being fully present in the moment. Mindfulness allows us to pause, reflect, and make conscious decisions rather than acting on autopilot. By cultivating awareness, we gain clarity about our values and priorities, enabling us to align our actions with our purpose.

In Buddhist philosophy, mindfulness is seen as a path to liberation. The *Satipatthana Sutta*, one of the foundational texts on mindfulness, teaches that by observing our thoughts, emotions, and actions with nonjudgmental awareness, we can free ourselves from habitual patterns and live with greater intention. This principle applies not only to spiritual practice but also to everyday life, where mindfulness helps us focus on what truly matters.

Consider the simple act of choosing how to spend your time. Without mindfulness, it is easy to become consumed by distractions or obligations that do not align with your values. Mindfulness creates the space to ask, "Does this choice reflect what is most important to me?" This question serves as a compass, guiding your actions toward your long-term purpose.

Proactive Decision-Making: The Key to Intention

Living with intention also requires proactive decision-making—the ability to act with purpose rather than merely reacting to circumstances. Proactivity involves setting clear goals, identifying priorities, and taking deliberate steps to achieve them. It is the opposite of passivity, where external forces dictate our actions.

One practical tool for proactive decision-making is the practice of setting daily intentions. At the start of each day, take a few moments to reflect on your goals and values. Ask yourself, "What do I want to focus on today?" and "How can my actions contribute to my larger purpose?" Writing down your intentions helps solidify them, creating a roadmap for the day.

Another strategy is to establish rituals that support your purpose. For instance, if one of your goals is to strengthen your relationships, you might create a habit of reaching out to a loved one each week. If personal growth is a priority, you could dedicate time each day to reading or learning. These rituals anchor your actions in intention, ensuring that your efforts align with your aspirations.

The Role of Small, Meaningful Actions

Living with intention does not require grand gestures or sweeping changes. Often, it is the small, consistent actions that have the most significant impact. These actions, when aligned with your values, create a cumulative effect that shapes your legacy over time.

Consider the story of Rosa Parks, whose decision to refuse giving up her bus seat became a pivotal moment in the American civil rights movement. Parks' action was not spontaneous;

it reflected years of intentional living rooted in her commitment to justice and equality. Her small but courageous act exemplifies how deliberate choices, no matter how modest, can lead to profound change.

In everyday life, small acts of kindness, generosity, and gratitude contribute to a meaningful legacy. A teacher who takes the time to encourage a struggling student, a neighbor who offers support in times of need, or a colleague who fosters collaboration—all of these actions, though seemingly ordinary, reflect intentional living that leaves a lasting impact.

The Intersection of Intention and Purpose

When we live with intention, we create a bridge between our daily actions and our larger purpose. This alignment brings a sense of coherence and fulfillment to our lives. For example, a healthcare worker who views their role as a way to serve others may find deep meaning in their daily interactions with patients, even in the face of challenges. Their intentional approach transforms routine tasks into expressions of their purpose.

Similarly, artists, entrepreneurs, and activists who live with intention often describe their work as an extension of their values and passions. By connecting their actions to their purpose, they infuse their lives with energy and meaning, inspiring others to do the same.

Overcoming Obstacles to Intentional Living

Despite its benefits, living with intention can be challenging. Modern life is filled with distractions, competing demands, and societal pressures that pull us away from our values. Overcoming these obstacles requires self-awareness and resilience.

One common barrier is the fear of failure or judgment. Choosing to live with intention often means taking risks, whether it is pursuing a passion, speaking out for what you believe in, or breaking away from conventional paths. Recognizing that failure is a natural part of growth can help you stay committed to your purpose.

Another challenge is the tendency to equate

busyness with productivity. Living with intention means prioritizing what truly matters, even if it means letting go of less essential tasks. This shift requires courage and discipline but ultimately leads to a more meaningful and balanced life.

Conclusion

Living with intention is a practice that transforms ordinary moments into opportunities for purpose and significance. By cultivating mindfulness, making proactive choices, and aligning your actions with your values, you create a life that reflects what matters most to you. Let each day be a step toward your larger purpose, a chance to contribute to your legacy through deliberate and meaningful action. In doing so, you not only enrich your own life but also inspire others to live with intention, creating a ripple effect of purpose and connection.

Making a Lasting Impact

A lasting impact is not measured by the magnitude of one's actions but by the depth of their resonance. It is created through a life of service, kindness, and intentional contributions that align with one's values. To leave a meaningful legacy is to inspire others, touch lives, and foster positive change in ways that endure beyond our time. This section explores the lessons of history's great figures and the practical steps we can take to make a lasting mark on the world.

Service as the Foundation of Legacy

Service is at the heart of leaving a meaningful impact. Mahatma Gandhi, who dedicated his life to fighting for India's independence and the principles of nonviolence, exemplified this truth. Gandhi's philosophy of *satyagraha*—holding steadfast to truth—was not merely a strategy for political resistance but a way of life grounded in service to humanity. His legacy endures not because of wealth or power but because of his unwavering commitment to justice and compassion.

Gandhi's life teaches us that acts of service, no matter how small, have the potential to create ripples of change. Whether advocating for social reform, volunteering in your community, or simply offering a helping hand to someone in need, service connects us to others and amplifies our influence. By focusing on the well-being of others, we transcend the limitations of individual ambition, contributing to a collective legacy of kindness and unity.

The Power of Kindness and Humility

Kindness and humility are perhaps the most universal and enduring ways to leave a positive mark. The Roman philosopher Seneca emphasized the importance of extending goodwill to others, regardless of their status or circumstances. In his writings, he argued that acts of kindness reflect the strength of one's character and create bonds of trust and reciprocity that outlast fleeting achievements.

In modern times, figures like Fred Rogers, the beloved host of *Mister Rogers' Neighborhood*, have demonstrated the transformative power of kindness. Rogers' gentle, empathetic approach to addressing complex emotions and challenges left an indelible impression on generations of viewers. His legacy reminds us that even small, consistent acts of care—listening with intent, offering encouragement, or creating safe spaces for others—can shape lives and communities.

Humility also plays a critical role in fostering meaningful connections and inspiring others. By acknowledging our shared humanity and embracing the contributions of others, we create an environment of mutual respect and collaboration. Humble leaders, teachers, and mentors often leave the most lasting legacies, not because they seek recognition but because they empower those around them to thrive.

Building Contributions Through Consistency

Leaving a lasting impact does not require extraordinary actions; it often arises from consistent, purposeful effort over time. The Japanese concept of *kaizen*, or continuous improvement, emphasizes the value of small, incremental changes that accumulate into significant results. Whether in personal growth, relationships, or professional endeavors, consistent contributions build trust, resilience, and progress.

Consider the example of Jane Goodall, whose decades-long work in wildlife conservation has transformed global attitudes toward animals and the environment. Goodall's legacy is not just her groundbreaking research on chimpanzees but her consistent advocacy for sustainable living and compassion for all creatures. Her work demonstrates that enduring impact is often the result of sustained commitment to a cause, driven by a clear sense of purpose.

In our own lives, we can apply this principle by identifying the areas where we can make a difference and committing to regular, meaningful action. Whether it's mentoring a colleague, volunteering for a local initiative, or dedicating time to personal development, these consistent efforts create a foundation for lasting impact.

Inspiring Others Through Example

The most profound legacies are those that inspire others to carry forward our values and ideals. By leading through example, we demonstrate that ethical living, service, and resilience are not abstract concepts but attainable practices. This inspiration creates a ripple effect, empowering others to take up the torch and continue the work we have begun.

One of the most powerful examples of this dynamic is Dr. Martin Luther King Jr., whose leadership in the civil rights movement ignited a global commitment to justice and equality. King's speeches, writings, and actions continue to inspire individuals and movements worldwide, reminding us that our influence can extend far beyond our immediate circle.

We, too, can inspire others by living authentically and courageously, embodying the principles we wish to see in the world. Whether through mentorship, storytelling, or simply living with integrity, our example becomes a source of encouragement and guidance for those who follow.

Practical Steps for Making a Lasting Impact

Leaving a legacy begins with small, intentional steps. One effective approach is to identify a cause or community that aligns with your values and dedicate time, energy, or resources to its advancement. Whether it's supporting education, advocating for social justice, or fostering environmental sustainability, your contributions create tangible and intangible benefits that endure.

Journaling and reflection can also play a role in guiding your efforts. By regularly assessing your actions and their alignment with your values, you can ensure that your contributions remain meaningful and impactful. Asking questions like "How have I made a difference this week?" or "What can I do to support others?" keeps your focus on creating positive change.

Another powerful practice is to cultivate gratitude and recognition for the contributions of others. By celebrating and amplifying the work of those around you, you create a culture of appreciation and collaboration, reinforcing the values you wish to promote.

Legacy Through Creativity and Innovation

For many, creativity and innovation offer unique avenues for leaving a mark. Artists, writers, and thinkers contribute to the cultural and intellectual fabric of society, inspiring future generations through their work. Consider the enduring influence of figures like Leonardo da Vinci or Maya Angelou, whose creations continue to resonate across time and space.

Even in fields like science, technology, and entrepreneurship, innovation driven by a commitment to the greater good can create lasting change. Think of Marie Curie's groundbreaking discoveries in radioactivity or Elon Musk's efforts to revolutionize sustainable energy and space exploration. These legacies remind us that our contributions can take many forms, each offering the potential to shape the future.

Conclusion

Making a lasting impact is not about fame or fortune; it is about living a life of purpose, service, and integrity. By focusing on kindness, consistency, and meaningful contributions, we can leave behind a legacy that uplifts and inspires others. Whether through small acts of service or bold innovations, the mark we leave is a reflection of our values and aspirations. Let this commitment to making a difference guide your actions, reminding you that the impact of a life well-lived extends far beyond its duration.

CONCLUSION: EMBRACING THE WISDOM OF THE EVERYDAY PHILOSOPHER

As we arrive at the end of this journey, it is worth pausing to reflect on the threads that have woven together the tapestry of insights explored in this book. The *Everyday Philosopher* is not a distant ideal but a role each of us can assume. It is a practice, a mindset, and a way of being that transforms the mundane into the meaningful, the ordinary into the extraordinary. This journey has not only illuminated timeless truths but also offered practical ways to integrate them into the fabric of daily life.

The overarching narrative of this book is clear: within each challenge, routine, and moment of introspection lies an opportunity for growth, connection, and purpose. By adopting the principles of resilience, mindfulness, balance, and ethical living, we create lives that are not only meaningful to ourselves but also profoundly impactful on others. Let us revisit and amplify these lessons, carrying them forward as a source of inspiration and guidance.

The Power of Perspective

It is often said that we cannot control the circumstances of life, but we can always control how we respond to them. From the wisdom of Epictetus to the groundbreaking insights of Viktor Frankl, we have learned that perspective is the key to shaping our reality. By reframing challenges as opportunities for growth and embracing gratitude for the present moment, we cultivate a mindset that is both resilient and hopeful.

The lesson here is simple yet transformative: the way we see the world determines the way we experience it. By shifting our perspective, we unlock the ability to navigate adversity with grace and to find meaning even in the face of difficulty.

The Art of Balance

Modern life often pulls us in conflicting directions, leaving us overwhelmed and disconnected. Yet, the principles of balance, drawn from the Taoist concept of Yin-Yang and Aristotle's *Golden Mean*, remind us that harmony lies not in perfection but in the dynamic interplay of opposites. Balance is not a static state but an ongoing practice—one that requires us to prioritize, reflect, and adjust as circumstances evolve.

Incorporating rest and renewal, setting boundaries, and integrating mindful routines into daily life allow us to create a foundation for sustainable well-being. Through balance, we reclaim our energy and focus, enabling us to thrive amidst the complexities of a busy world.

Building Resilience

Resilience is the quiet strength that carries us through life's storms. The stories of Nietzsche, Frankl, and the Japanese philosophy of kintsugi have shown us that adversity, while painful, can also be transformative. The cracks and imperfections we accumulate are not flaws but evidence of growth and reinvention.

Resilience is not just about enduring hardship; it is about emerging from it stronger and more purposeful. By embracing tools like self-reflection, mindfulness, and supportive practices, we build the inner fortitude to thrive no matter what life throws our way.

The Discipline of Habits

Habits shape our character and, ultimately, our destiny. Aristotle's wisdom that "we are what we repeatedly do" reminds us of the profound impact of our daily actions. Positive habits, cultivated through consistency and intentionality, serve as the building blocks of a fulfilling life.

Breaking unproductive patterns and sustaining discipline require patience and self-compassion. Yet, the rewards are immense: a life aligned with our values, where our actions reflect the person we aspire to be.

Ethical Living and Meaningful Connections

At the heart of a life well-lived lies the ability to connect deeply—with ourselves, with others, and with the world around us. Ethical living, guided by frameworks like Kant's categorical imperative and the relational wisdom of Martin Buber, challenges us to align our actions with our values. In doing so, we create relationships rooted in trust, empathy, and integrity.

Living ethically and fostering meaningful connections enrich not only our lives but also the lives of those we touch. By navigating conflict with grace and leading by example, we become catalysts for positive change, inspiring others to do the same.

The Legacy You Leave

Legacy is the sum of the lives we touch and the values we embody. It is not reserved for the extraordinary; it is created in the quiet moments of kindness, courage, and service. From Gandhi's nonviolent resistance to Seneca's meditations on virtue, history shows us that our actions, no matter how small, ripple outward in ways we cannot fully comprehend.

By living with intention, aligning our daily choices with our larger purpose, and embracing a mindset of contribution, we craft legacies that endure. Each of us has the power to leave behind a world that is kinder, stronger, and more compassionate because we were part of it.

The Journey Ahead

As this book draws to a close, it is important to recognize that the journey of the *Everyday Philosopher* does not end here. The insights and practices shared in these pages are not meant to be static lessons but living principles—ones that evolve as you grow and as the world around you changes.

The path forward is yours to define. Perhaps it begins with a small act of kindness, a moment of reflection, or the courage to embrace a new perspective. Whatever steps you take, remember that philosophy is not an abstract ideal; it is a way of living, thinking, and being that empowers you to find meaning and fulfillment in every aspect of life.

A Final Call to Action

Let this moment be an invitation to pause and reflect. What will you do with the insights you have gained? How will you apply them to your own life? What legacy do you wish to leave?

You hold the power to transform your life and the lives of those around you. By embracing the wisdom of the *Everyday Philosopher*, you become a beacon of resilience, compassion, and purpose—a force for good in a world that desperately needs it.

The journey may not always be easy, but it is always worth it. As you step forward, carry these words with you: Live thoughtfully. Act courageously. Love deeply. And remember, the most profound wisdom is not found in books or lectures but in the way you choose to live each day. This is your legacy, your gift to the world. Make it extraordinary.

ACKNOWLEDGEMENT

Creating *The Everyday Philosopher* has been an extraordinary journey, and it would not have been possible without the support, inspiration, and contributions of many remarkable individuals.

To the timeless thinkers—Aristotle, Epictetus, Seneca, and so many others—your enduring wisdom forms the foundation of this work. Your teachings continue to guide and inspire generations, and I am humbled to bring your insights into today's world.

To my readers, thank you for your curiosity, courage, and commitment to personal growth. Your journey fuels the purpose of this book, and it is an honor to walk this path with you.

To my close friends and family, your unwavering encouragement and belief in this project kept me grounded and motivated. Your love and support remind me of the power of meaningful connections.

Finally, to those who work tirelessly to preserve and share the wisdom of the past—scholars, translators, and educators—this book stands on the shoulders of your dedication. Thank you for keeping the flame of knowledge alive.

This book is as much yours as it is mine. My deepest gratitude to all who made it possible.

ABOUT THE AUTHOR

Felix Grayson's journey into timeless wisdom began in childhood, captivated by the stories of philosophers, leaders, and visionaries who shaped the way we think and live. Growing up in a home filled with books, he spent countless hours exploring ideas that asked life's biggest questions—a curiosity that would later define his work.

After facing his own modern challenges—balancing ambition, uncertainty, and the search for meaning—Felix discovered that the wisdom of the past offers profound guidance for the present. This realization became the foundation for the *Stoned Philosopher* series: a collection dedicated to translating ancient insights into practical lessons for today's world.

Felix's writing is more than reflection—it's an invitation to dialogue with history's greatest minds. Through each book, he helps readers find clarity, resilience, and purpose in their own lives—one timeless idea at a time.

When not writing, Felix enjoys quiet contemplation, deep conversation, and exploring the endless pursuit of wisdom in everyday moments.